D0339037

THE RISEN CHRIST
IN THE FATHERS OF THE CHURCH

BOARD OF EDITORS

John E. Lynch, C.S.P. (General Editor)
Professor of Church History
St. Paul's College

Thomas P. Collins
Instructor in Theology
Manhattan College

Johannes Quasten
Professor of Ancient Church History
and Christian Archaeology
Catholic University of America

Wilfred F. Dewan, C.S.P.
Professor of Dogmatic Theology
St. Paul's College

Thomas F. Finn, C.S.P.
Professor of Sacramental Theology
St. Paul's College

Walter J. Burghardt, S.J.
Professor of Patristic Theology
Woodstock College

Eugene M. Burke, C.S.P.
Professor of Dogmatic Theology
Catholic University of America

Gerard S. Sloyan
Professor of Religious Education
Catholic University of America

THE RISEN CHRIST

in the
FATHERS OF THE CHURCH

Prepared and Edited

with

Introduction and Commentary

by

THOMAS P. COLLINS

PAULIST PRESS   GLEN ROCK, N. J.

NIHIL OBSTAT:
Robert E. Hunt, S.T.D.
Censor Librorum

IMPRIMATUR:
✝ Thomas A. Boland, S.T.D.
Archbishop of Newark

April 11, 1967

The Nihil Obstat and Imprimatur are official declarations that a book or pamphlet is free of doctrinal or moral error. No implication is contained therein that those who have granted the Nihil Obstat and Imprimatur agree with the contents, opinions or statements expressed.

Copyright © 1967 by
The Missionary Society
of St. Paul the Apostle
in the State of New York

Library of Congress
Catalog Card Number: 67–23608

Cover Design: Emil Antonucci

Published by Paulist Press
Editorial Office: 304 W. 58th St., N.Y., N.Y. 10019
Business Office: Glen Rock, New Jersey 07452

Printed and bound in the
United States of America

CONTENTS

Contents

PRENOTE

This modest survey of patristic materials on the resurrection of Christ is in no sense intended to present an exhaustive or even complete inventory of the fathers' writing on the subject. An exhaustive study would fill volumes. A complete survey would require far more research time than a busy teaching and publishing schedule permitted.

But I hope that this brief look at a vast and little cultivated field of patristic studies will serve to stimulate theology students who are as yet relatively unfamiliar with the sources. This survey is obviously not intended for patristic scholars. But teachers of theology may find here occasional indications of a problem or a viewpoint that had escaped their notice.

An attempt has been made within the limits of available material and of a chronological framework to highlight some issues that are especially important to our own time. Here the study admittedly becomes controversial, and the discussion questions will indicate some of the issues on which my viewpoint may readily be challenged.

What follows is ultimately my sole responsibility. I would like, however, to give special thanks to those who were of greatest help to me: to Brother Luke Salm, F.S.C., of Manhattan College where I taught from 1963-66; to the librarians at Union Theological Seminary who provided ready access to books not available elsewhere; to Dr. M. J. Donnelly who was extremely helpful in his criticism and his assistance with the final manuscript. Most of all, I would like to thank my wife, who by her constant help, encouragement and questioning has made possible whatever small achievement this book represents.

Thomas P. Collins

LIST OF ABBREVIATIONS

ACW   Ancient Christian Writers, ed. J. Quasten et al. Westminster, Md., 1946ff.

ANF   Ante-Nicene Fathers. Buffalo and New York.

Bettenson   H. Bettenson, ed., The Early Christian Fathers. New York and London, 1956.

Bonner   C. Bonner, ed., The Homily on the Passion by Melito of Sardis. London, 1940.

Dix   G. Dix, ed., Treatise on the Apostolic Tradition. London, 1937.

Drewery   B. Drewery, Origen and the Doctrine of Grace. London, 1960.

ECD   J. N. D. Kelly, Early Christian Doctrines. New York, 1960.

Greer   R. Greer, Theodore of Mopsuestia. London, 1961.

IWG   The Incarnation of the Word of God. New York, 1951.

LCC   Library of Christian Classics: Treatises in Controversy with the Arians. Oxford, 1844.

LFC   Library of the Fathers of the Holy Catholic Church, ed. E. Pusey et al. Oxford, 1838-88.

Norris   R. A. Norris, Manhood and Christ. Oxford, 1963.

NPNF   Nicene and Post-Nicene Fathers. New York.

PG   Migne, Patrologia Graeca.

Quasten   J. Quasten, Patrology I-III. Westminster, Md., 1950ff.

Ramsey   A. M. Ramsey, The Resurrection of Christ. London, 1956.

Srawley   J. H. Srawley, St. Ambrose on the Sacraments and on the Mysteries. Bungay, Suffolk, 1950.

Weller   P. T. Weller, ed., Selected Easter Sermons of St. Augustine. London, 1959.

Williams   A. L. Williams, tr., Justin Martyr, The Dialogue with Trypho. London, 1931.

GENERAL INTRODUCTION

John Henry Newman in his *Lectures on the Doctrine of Justification* speaks of

> a peculiarity of the apostles' preaching, which has sometimes caused remark. They insist on our Lord's resurrection, as if it were the main doctrine of the gospel; but why so, and not on his divinity or the atonement? Many good reasons may be given for this; as, for instance, that the resurrection was the great miracle and evidence of the divinity of the religion; or that it is the pledge of our resurrection; on the other hand, that his divinity and atonement were doctrines too sacred to preach to the world. But if . . . the resurrection be the means by which the atonement is applied to each of us, if it be our justification, if in it are conveyed all the gifts of grace and glory which Christ has purchased for us, if it be the commencement of his giving himself to us for our spiritual sustenance, of his feeding us with that bread which has already been perfected on the cross, and is now a medicine of immortality, it is that very doctrine which is most immediate to us, in which Christ most closely approaches us, from which we gain life, and out of which issue our hopes and our duties. Christ is God from everlasting; he became man under Caesar Augustus; he was an atonement for the world on the cross; but he became a savior on his resurrection (London, 1914, pp. 221-22).

The resurrection of Christ from the dead is either stated or implied in every book of the New Testament, beginning with Acts and the letters of Paul. From the resurrection-event directly spring, in their uniqueness, Christian faith, Christian preaching, Christian theology, Christian worship and Christian ethics.

In his resurrection Christ is constituted Lord and Son; it is arguable that it is at the resurrection that the Holy Spirit enters history and the Christian Church is established as the new

1

People of God. The resurrrection of Christ sheds light backward and forward on all history, penetrating to the very origins of man and looking forward to man's ultimate fulfillment.

With the help of the New Testament and the fathers, we can mark a double revelation in the key event of the resurrection. First comes a revelation that centers upon the person of Christ; second, a revelation that illumines the meaning and destiny of man in Christ.

1. One of the most important features of the resurrection, then, is its revelation of the meaning of the person of Christ. For example, the resurrection makes it impossible to see the story of Christ's life and death as a tragic story. Instead, the resurrection retrospectively reveals the Christ who lived and died as a person of whom divinity itself could be predicated. So powerful an effect did this event have on the disciples of Christ, that they, who in his passion had dissociated themselves from him, who at his death and burial were plunged into despair, suddenly emerged to justify in the face of all Jerusalem "Jesus of Nazareth, whom you crucified, whom God raised from the dead. . . . This was the stone which was rejected by you builders, but which has become the head of the corner. And there is salvation in no one else, for there is no other name under heaven given among men by which we must be saved" (Acts 4:10-12). This fact they proclaimed as the certain and unassailable basis of Christian existence: "If Christ has not been raised, then our preaching is in vain and your faith is in vain. . . . If Christ has not been raised, your faith is futile and you are still in your sins" (1 Cor 15:14. 17).

In the accounts of the resurrection and resurrection-appearances given in the gospels and Acts 1, the concern of the authors is to reassert and "document" the event, the *fact*. The New Testament writers attempt no philosophical or psychological explanation of *how* Christ rose, or how he was able to manifest himself, or how those to whom he appeared knew him. He was obviously the same person they had known before the passion, the same person who had died and been buried. He was no ghost. He ate, drank, cooked; they touched him and saw him. He was really, bodily present. They were not interested in psychic or parapsychic explanations of how all this took place. It was sufficient to know that he was physically risen, and that this was God's act—that it was accomplished by the Father in him, that Father who came to be defined in the New Testament as the God who raised Jesus from the dead (Rom 4:24).

What did this fact mean? It meant that Jesus was Lord, was in his resurrection born as Son of God. It meant that he was judge, mediator, high priest, image of God in the full sense, light of the world, resurrection and life, Word, savior, bread of life.

2. Yet we would make a mistake—supported neither by the New Testament nor by the fathers—if we were to see the resurrection of Christ as an event which happened for Christ's sake alone. His resurrection was and is the event by which he redeems; and if we examine any of the above titles or "names," we shall see that what Christ is in virtue of his resurrection, he is in relation to man and creation. Far from Christ alone being affected by his resurrection, all creation is affected. All reality somehow is or is to be redeemed. For this the resurrection of man is crucial: "The creation waits with eager longing for the revealing of the sons of God . . . because creation itself will be set free from its bondage to decay and obtain the glorious liberty of the children of God" (Rom 8:19. 21).

In the New Testament the resurrection of man is not only a matter of otherworldly, everlasting life. What the resurrection of man in Christ means is not only a deliverance from physical death into eternal life. It also means—and this is in some ways more primary—the here-and-now deliverance of man from spiritual death into a life lived in Christ and in consciousness of the power of his resurrection. It is as a matter of fact the experience of the risen Lord and his power through faith that in this life constitutes the *only* authentic Christian knowledge of the resurrection. The Christian does not know resurrection as some kind of immortality of the soul proposed to him as a posthumous reward for meritorious behavior. Rather, the fundamental Christian idea of the resurrection begins with the experience of lived union with the risen Lord here and now and, through personal trust in the living Jesus, is known to be a union in life forever. Not all have experienced the victory of Christ as something in which they themselves are involved. That is why the Gospel is preached—so that men may know here and now that they share in Christ's resurrection and so that they may now live within his resurrection and within his divine life. Ultimately, somehow, all men will come to know him and the power of his resurrection, "so that God may be everything to everyone" (1 Cor. 15:28). This is the meaning of history, the project of history: "As in Adam all die, so also in Christ shall all be made alive" (1 Cor 15:22).

Meantime there is the opportunity of baptism into Christ through which men who believe in him put off what is not Christ and put on Christ, die to sin and, "just as Christ was raised from the dead through the glory of the Father" (Rom 6:4), also now walk in newness of life. Resurrection for these people is not something in the future. They are now "dead to sin and alive to God in Christ Jesus" (Rom 5:11). They have already passed from death to life (1 Jn 3:14). They possess within themselves the pledge and foretaste of final resurrection. They already experience this resurrection through Christ's Spirit who dwells in them (cf. Rom 8:11).

"In Christ shall all be made alive" (1 Cor 15:22). This is, then, a man who in his flesh was victorious on man's behalf not only over sin and death but in achieving newness of life. Some of the fathers, as we shall see, liked to apply to Christ a phrase (which we now know to be a misquotation) from Psalm 88: Christ was "free among the dead" (cf. Ps 88:5). The point is valid and illuminating: Christ rose to total perfection as man and thus to total freedom. But more than that, the point is designed as a pointer for men: In his resurrection they also rise and will rise to perfect freedom. In this, as in other cases, the truth about the risen Lord is a truth about men—about their lordship, their dominion. The victory of Christ is nothing else than the victory of man, because it is a man who is risen and risen *as man*. He is firstborn among the dead as the first of *men* to be born as divine Son. This means that all other men are called to share divine sonship with him, to be, like him, God's sons. "And if sons, then heirs also—God's heirs and co-heirs with Christ" (Rom 8:17).

And here we have an aspect of Christ's resurrection that is coming fully into view only in our own time. Christ is risen that man may rise. His risen lordship is the reign of a man, the dominion of a man, the first event in the age of the dominion of mankind. Whatever other norms we use for human dominion— the condition in which man is fully in control as man—a Christian must measure it above all according to the fullness of the maturity of the living Christ. This dominion of man achieved once for all in Christ must, in the individual, the Christian community and the human race, be worked out in time. Yet the fact itself that he is risen can be taken as a pledge of the coming dominion of mankind, as a sign that history—the history of man in solidarity with Christ's own personal history—will end by the power of God in resurrection and life. In other words, it would seem from the very thrust of Christ's history—since Christ is pioneer, forerunner of all men—that human history must and can be only a drive toward risen life. Otherwise Christ's history would not fully be the paradigm of man's. Otherwise, too, Christ's victory would remain in some sense incomplete.

Paul's hope for the Christian community expresses the Christian hope for man—for the past, the present and (in a special way) the future of mankind. It is the hope that he who raised up Jesus Christ will raise man up also. It is the hope that he will bring the race of men, as well as the individual person and the community of Christians, to the measure of the stature of the maturity of Christ.

Thus the mystery of the resurrection of Jesus Christ provides the paradigm of what the future of man can be—what the Christian lives in hope that it shall be: a progress toward risen human life, toward human dominion and man's divinization after the pattern of Christ's risen lordship and in virtue of his living presence in divine power among men. In this hope, the future of man is seen as a dynamic evolutionary movement toward increasingly greater and more perfect maturity in the context of his transformed and deified humanity. To put it another way, Christians today have no message more central or more important to give to mankind: He lives, and you shall live.

In the following pages we shall examine the Christian literature of the first five centuries. We shall see some highlights of the writers' responses to the New Testament teaching about the resurrection of Christ. We shall see that they view the resurrection as a mystery in which man is involved—and man's destiny.

QUESTIONS FOR DISCUSSION

1. What place does the fact of Christ's resurrection hold in the writings of the New Testament?
2. Discuss the double revelation contained in the resurrection of Christ.
3. In the accounts of the resurrection and the resurrection-appearances, did the authors attempt to explain *how* Christ rose or how he was able to manifest himself? Explain. What did the resurrection of Christ mean for these writers?
4. What is the significance of Christ's resurrection for man and creation? How are people here and now affected by this event?
5. In what does authentic Christian knowledge of the resurrection consist?
6. Does the resurrection mean, for the Christian, immortality of soul as a posthumous reward? Explain your answer.
7. In the author's view, why is the Gospel preached? What is the significance of baptism in this context?
8. When some of the fathers applied the phrase "free among the dead" (cf. Ps 88), what were they indicating? What significance does this have for men? Discuss.
9. Does Christ's history tell man anything about human history? Explain.
10. In what sense is the resurrection of Christ "the first event in the age of the dominion of mankind"? What does this mean? How does a Christian measure human dominion? How can Christ's resurrection be called a paradigm for the future of mankind?

CHAPTER 1

APOCALYPSE

AND ALLEGORY

Prefatory Note

From the time of the New Testament, Christ's resurrection had been asserted in credal statements as an essential of Christian faith. We may think of creeds as abstract formulae, but from the dawn of Christianity—e.g., in St. Paul's writings to the Romans—confession of Christ was confession in rich awareness of a known person. Paul preaches the Good News of God as "the Gospel of his Son, who was descended from David according to the flesh and designated Son of God in power according to the Spirit of holiness by his resurrection from the dead, Jesus Christ our Lord, through whom we have received grace and apostleship. . . ." (Rom 1:3-5). Moreover, in the earliest formal credal texts we have (deriving from the apostles but formulated in "articles" afterward), Christ's resurrection is always juxtaposed with the resurrection of man, as in Hippolytus' *Apostolic Tradition:* "I believe in God . . . and in Christ Jesus, Son of God, who . . . rose on the third day, living from among the dead . . . and in the resurrection of the flesh."

Also prominent in early formal creeds was the idea of Christ as judge of living and dead. This was connected closely with his emergence as one living from among the dead, and was an emphasis whose urgency came not so much from the New Testament (other stresses were equally or more marked in the Gospel) as from the imminent expectation of a general judgment following a sudden and catastrophic collapse of the present world and the second coming of Christ. This was a mistake. Yet Christ's preaching is so treated by the evangelists as to stress this expectation: Paul's early preaching shows it, and the New Testament Apocalypse or Book of Revelation is, as we shall see, by no means the last Christian writing to emphasize it. Here we have something of the context for the *Didache* selection below, a specimen whose tone might surprise us were we not aware of the excitement and confusion generated by this expectation of Christ's coming and judgment. Clement's letter which follows is (except for its analogical sections) more in harmony with the main theological and emotional thrust of the Gospel; still more in harmony are the letters of Ignatius (in the following chapter) which richly sum up New Testament Christology, particularly that of Paul and John. And so we turn to one of the earliest extant samples of post-apostolic writing, a passage from the conclusion of the *Didache*.

1. THE DIDACHE

Introduction

The *Didache,* or "the Lord's *Instruction* to the Gentiles through the Twelve Apostles," is a collection (dated as early as 70-90) of Church regulations and liturgical and catechetical material by an unknown compiler, probably a Syrian. As indicated above, the passage is heavily eschatological (or "end-times" oriented), in keeping with the conviction, widespread among early Christians, that Christ's cosmic second coming was proximate. What puts the selection in the genre of "apocalypse" (like the Old Testament Book of Daniel or the New Testament Book of Revelation) are such features as its mystic quality, its deliverance of a "secret," its oracular focus on the circumstances of the end of the world and its very dependence on Old Testament and New Testament apocalyptic writing.

An Apocalyptic Judge

Watch over your life; your lamps must not go out, nor your loins be ungirded; on the contrary, be ready. You do not know the hour in which our Lord is coming. . . . Then humankind will undergo the fiery test, and many will lose their faith and perish; but those who stand firm in their faith will be saved by none other than the accursed one. And then the proofs of the truth will appear; the first proof, an opening in the heavens; the next proof, the sounding of the trumpet; and the third, the resurrection of the dead—not of all indeed, but in accordance with the saying: The Lord will come and all the saints with him.

Finally, the world will behold the Lord riding the clouds in the
sky.   (Didache 16: based on ACW 6.24-25)

Commentary: Four eschatological themes found in many other
early Christian writings are evident here: Christ's *parousia* (his
glorious return or second coming in majesty); the resurrection
"of the saints"; judgment; and a catastrophic breakup of the
world order amid apocalyptic signs. Note the identification of
the coming of the Lord in power with the coming of his risen
saints (quite reminiscent of the Son of man texts in Dan. 7:13-
14 and Zech 14:5 with their many New Testament echoes). Also
worthy of note is the fact that Christ seemingly described here
(in view of his passion) as "the accursed one" has many titles
which can only be consequent upon his resurrection. Here the
titles would be "Lord," and (by implication) "judge" and "Son
of man" (in its full meaning). Christ's resurrection was the event
that made it possible to affirm of him without qualification the
fullness of divinity.

2. CLEMENT OF ROME

Introduction

Clement, who may have known the apostles Peter and Paul, was
listed by Irenaeus and Eusebius as the third successor of Peter at
Rome. Clement wrote this letter about the year 100. His reason for
writing to Corinth is like the reason for many another bishop's letter
in the patristic era: He is trying to quell a religious disturbance.

We note in Clement's letter, as in the *Didache* and most other
patristic writing, that the author's text is full of scriptural echoes.
Clement is eager to supply analogies for Christ's and the Christian's
resurrection by employing a variety of "nature" metaphors. Clement
elsewhere applies to the resurrection the phoenix mythology so
familiar in ancient literature from Hesiod to Ovid to Tacitus.

Images of the Resurrection

Let us consider, beloved, how the Master continually calls our
attention to the future resurrection, the first fruits of which he

has made the Lord Jesus Christ by raising him from the dead. Let us consider, beloved, the kind of resurrection that occurs at regular intervals. Day and night give us examples of resurrection. The night sleeps, the day rises; the day departs, the night comes on. Let us take the crops. The sowing—how and in what manner does it take place? The sower goes out and puts each of the seeds into the soil: when they fall on the soil, they are dry and bare, and decay. But once they have decayed, the Master's wondrous providence makes them rise, and each one increases and brings forth multiple fruit.

(Letter to the Corinthians 24-27: based on ACW 1.24-26)

Commentary: In the fathers, Christ is presented not only under titles and names which disclose rich facets of his risen lordship, but we also get images, sometimes very strange images, which verge on the absurd. Nor does the use of scripture always seem quite appropriate to us: Clement does not look quite legitimate in his employment of Old Testament "sayings." Yet something of the awesome splendor of the idea of the resurrection is communicated by his images. There is something of the perfect "reasonableness" of personal resurrection as answering man's age-old hope for life as the aftermath of death's night or sleep.

Resurrection and Mission

And so, after receiving their instructions and being fully assured through the resurrection of our Lord Jesus Christ, as well as confirmed in faith by the Word of God, they [the apostles] went forth, equipped with the fullness of the Holy Spirit, to preach the good news that the kingdom of God was close at hand. (Letter to the Corinthians 42.3: based on ACW 1.34-35)

Commentary: Clement shows the dependency of Christian apostolate or mission on the "full assurance" provided by the resurrection of Christ: The apostles are called out of hiding and joyously sped on their way by a force very powerful and illuminating to them. The confident optimism reminds us of the early chapters of Acts. In Clement, then, the resurrection is seen as conferring profound conviction. It motivates creative people to live and act enthusiastically within the context of the "Good News." We also note that here "the resurrection of our Lord Jesus" is seen as the central motivating event in the creative activity of living apostles; the resurrection of Christ serves not only as the exemplar for life in the world to come but as a compelling influence on and catalyst for life here and now.

QUESTIONS FOR DISCUSSION

1. Did the early Christians think of creeds as abstract formulae? Discuss their attitude.
2. What are some of the characteristics of early formal creeds?
3. In what ways is the selection from the *Didache* in the apocalyptic genre? What four eschatological themes found in many other early Christian writings are evident here? How is Christ's resurrection seen in this context?
4. How does Clement of Rome treat the fact of Christ's resurrection?
5. Clement speaks of the apostles as being "fully assured" by the resurrection of Christ. Explain the significance of this statement.

CHAPTER 2

LIFE AND DEATH

IN THE LIVING CHRIST

Introduction

Ignatius, bishop of Antioch, views Christ's resurrection as do
few other Christian witnesses. For him it is an intensely personal
event, igniting in man an almost explosive sense of the presence
of divine power. It is a lived reality which not only makes the
Christian person confident but transforms him. To me, to live
means Christ, Ignatius says with Paul—and some think he says
this more forcefully than Paul. Concern for Christ taught Ignatius
concern for Christian unity, and for the factual physical reality
of Christ which he maintained against docetists, who said that
Christ only *seemed* to have a body, to suffer and die and rise.

Ignatius' letters have been described as "warm, rich, exuberant,
generous, mystical." The seven letters all seem to have been written
while Ignatius was en route to martyrdom in Rome; his purpose
in the letter to the Romans is to confirm his fellow Christians in
the face of imminent persecution (by Trajan: 110-117), in which
Ignatius himself died.

The New Man, Jesus Christ

If Jesus Christ, yielding to your prayer, grants me the favor and
it is his will, I shall, in the subsequent letter which I intend to
write to you, still further explain the dispensation which I have
here only touched upon, regarding the new man, Christ Jesus—

13

a dispensation founded on faith in him and love for him, on his passion and resurrection.

(Letter to the Ephesians 20: based on ACW 1.67)

Commentary: The risen "Jesus Christ our God" (*Ephesians,* prologue) is seen as source of the dispensation initiated by the incarnation: with the birth of Christ "a star burst forth in the sky outshining all other stars. . . . God appeared in human form to mold the newness of eternal life" (*Ephesians* 19). Yet the dispensation is *founded on* the events of Christ's passion and resurrection: these are the Christic, objective correlates of subjective Christian faith and love.

An Established Fact

I merely wish to warn you betimes not to yield to the bait of false doctrine, but to believe most steadfastly in the birth, the passion, and the resurrection, which took place during the procuratorship of Pontius Pilate. Facts these are, real and established by Jesus Christ, our hope.

(Letter to the Magnesians 11: ACW 1.72-73)

Commentary: Ignatius insists upon unquestioned faith in the fact of the resurrection. The grouping together of birth and passion with the resurrection seems explicable only in view of a general denial of all physical factuality by some docetists. In any case, Ignatius offers no arguments, no explanations, no "proofs." The resurrection, like the other events, is factual. And it is a fact to be believed in.

"Who Will Raise Us Also"

. . . Mary's son, who was really born and ate and drank, really persecuted by Pontius Pilate, really crucified and died while heaven and earth and the underworld looked on; who also really rose from the dead, since his Father raised him up—his Father, who will likewise raise us also who believe in him through Jesus Christ, apart from whom we have no real life.

(Letter to the Trallians 9: ACW 1.77-78)

Commentary: Ignatius, like the New Testament authors, sometimes sees Christ as the agent of the resurrection; sometimes he attributes it to the Father. What is most important in this passage is the clear association of Christ's resurrection with the resurrection of the community of those who believe through Jesus Christ. A legitimate inference from the passage is that, for man, "real life," even in the present, can only be life in the risen Christ.

"Who Rose Again because of Us"

Of no use to me will be the farthest reaches of the universe or the kingdoms of this world. I would rather die and come to Jesus Christ than be king over the entire earth. Him I seek who died for us; him I love who rose again because of us. The birth pangs are upon me. Forgive me, brethren; do not obstruct my coming to life—do not wish me to die; do not make a gift to the world of one who wants to be God's. Beware of seducing me with matter; suffer me to receive pure light. Once arrived there I shall be a man. Permit me to be an imitator of my suffering God. . . .

I am writing while still alive, but my yearning is for death. My Love has been crucified, and I am not on fire with the love of earthly things. But there is in me a living water, which is eloquent and within me says: "Come to the Father."

(Letter to the Romans 6-7: ACW 1.83)

Commentary: In this most characteristically Ignatian letter, the author voices his fear that some Christians will try to get him a pardon or delay of execution. Since he is writing also to confirm the faith of his fellow Christians, Ignatius' most personal remarks have special meaning for the *Christian community,* and ultimately for the entire community of man. In other words, Ignatius writes not diary notes but public letters, in effect, urging *others* to "love him who rose again." This communal note is sometimes explicit: "Jesus Christ . . . rose again because of *us.*" Again, Christ's resurrection means risen life for man: "Do not obstruct my coming to life"; not to go to God, not to be born again to risen life after death, would be equivalent to death for him. Here, too, there is an early witness, consonant with later testimony, to a patristic theme derived from the New Testament Acts and letter to the Hebrews: Christ in his resurrection was born as Son and in him Christians also are reborn. Ignatius in effect says that, risen, the Christian is born as son. Again, also, to arrive at "pure light" through death is to attain the fullness of humanity—to attain to perfect human maturity. The motif of pure light as object shifts in the final phrases here to a motif of living water as springing up within the person (an image familiar from John's gospel: cf. 4:10; 7:28). The indwelling Christ, who is water (and fire) within the Christian, invites him, calls him, to divine union: "Come to the Father."

The Living Record

I exhort you never to act in a spirit of factiousness, but according to what you learned in the school of Christ. I heard some say, "Unless I find it in the official records ['the archives' of the Old Testament], I do not believe. [For I do not believe] in the Gospel." And when I answered them, "It is in the scriptures," they retorted: "That is just the point at issue." But to me the official record is Jesus Christ; the inviolable record is his cross and his death and his resurrection and the faith of which he is the author. These are the things which, thanks to your prayer, I want to be my justification.

(Letter to the Philadelphians 8: based on ACW 1.88)

Commentary: Ignatius seems to recognize, much better than certain Christian writers after him (see, for example, Justin, in chapter 5 below), that an apologetic built on scriptural argument cannot convince someone who is not really ready to see. Personal faith is the only sure way to know Christ, not argument from scripture. Not only that: The scriptures are themselves interpreted by more important archives; there is a more basic source of assurance—the person of Jesus Christ and events like the resurrection in which he left a memorial of what he was and what he did for man: "To me the official record is Jesus Christ." Ignatius is here very practical and economical in his use of "authorities": he cuts through secondary sources to get at the living ground of Christian existence.

Christ's Resurrection in the Flesh

For myself, I know and believe that he was in the flesh even after the resurrection. And when he came to Peter and Peter's companions, he said to them: "Here; feel me and see that I am not a bodiless ghost" [cf. Lk 24:30-43]. Immediately they touched him and, through this contact with his flesh and spirit, believed. For the same reason they despised death and, in fact, proved stronger than death. Again, after the resurrection, he ate and drank with them like a being of flesh and blood, though spiritually one with the Father.

(Letter to the Smyrnaeans 3: ACW 1.91)

Commentary: Ignatius (in *Smyrnaeans* 2) had said that "unbelievers" (docetists) who see a phantom Christ, a phantom death and resurrection, will reap the harvest of their unbelief: "And he suffered really, as he really raised himself from the dead. [As to] certain unbelievers . . . in fact, it is they who are unreal; and their end will be like their fantasies: they will turn out to be bodiless ghosts." Since these docetists denied the reality of Christ's flesh and bodily resurrection, they can expect no resurrection of their own bodies, Ignatius seems to argue.

In the present passage, Ignatius does not explain his belief in Christ's resurrection: this is an inarguable fact of faith. Rather, he gives reasons why Christ's resurrection is a resurrection of his *flesh* as well as of his spirit. Further, we note that for Ignatius contact with the risen Christ means a triumphant despising of death, now looked on not as an end but rather as the passage to fullness of life.

QUESTIONS FOR DISCUSSION

1. In what ways is Ignatius of Antioch a remarkable witness to the resurrection of Christ?
2. Why did Ignatius insist on the *fact* of the resurrection? What was his attitude toward arguments?
3. How does Ignatius understand the relation between the risen Christ and the Christian community?

4. A patristic theme derived from the New Testament is presented in Ignatius' letter to the Romans. What is this theme?
5. What is the basic source of assurance for personal faith? How does Ignatius express this?
6. Why does Ignatius of Antioch stress that Christ's resurrection is a resurrection of his *flesh?*

CHAPTER 3
JOY, REVELATION,
EVERLASTING LIFE

Prefatory Note

The letters that follow approach from different viewpoints the meaning of the resurrection in man's life. We can identify with reasonable assurance only the author of the first three letters.

1. POLYCARP

Introduction

Polycarp (d. 156), a contemporary and friend of Ignatius of Antioch, is associated repeatedly by Irenaeus with John the Evangelist. Ignatius had pictured a timid Polycarp in his early years as bishop. Yet, Polycarp became redoubtable enough to speak as testily as he does below. There is also a story that Polycarp was asked by Marcion (the gnostic) whether he recognized Marcion, and that Polycarp answered: "Of course I recognize the firstborn of Satan."

Scholars generally date the letter cited about the year 135. Polycarp's mentality is partly like that of Clement of Rome, partly like that of Ignatius of Antioch.

The God Who Raised Jesus

I also congratulate you on the fact that your firmly rooted faith, celebrated ever since the earliest days, persists till now and still brings forth fruit to the honor of our Lord Jesus Christ, who patiently went to meet his death for our sins—he whom God raised by ending the throes of death. You never saw him, and yet believe in him with sublime and inexpressible joy—a joy which many desire to experience. You are assured that you have been saved by a gratuitous gift, not by our actions—no, but by the will of God through Jesus Christ.

Therefore gird your loins and serve God in fear and in truth. . . . "Believe in him who raised our Lord Jesus Christ from the dead, and gave him glory" [1 Pet 1:21] and a throne at his right. To him all things in heaven and on earth were subjected; him every breathing creature worships; he is to come as the judge of the living and the dead; his blood God will avenge upon those that disobey him. Now, he who has raised him from the dead will raise us also, provided we do his will, make his commandments our rule of life, love what he loves, [and] abstain from every kind of wrongdoing. . . .

(Philippians 1-2: based on ACW 6.76)

Commentary: This letter includes a simple confession of faith in the resurrection of Christ. It shows the close connection, as in Clement and Ignatius, between Christ's resurrection, man's own resurrection and joyous Christian life. An important feature of this passage is the *triple* confession of the Father as the one who raised "our Lord Jesus Christ" from the dead. This reflects Paul's definition of God the Father as "him who raised our Lord from the dead." Hence the view that the object of Christian faith is not simply God, but God who raised up Christ, and that what distinguishes Jews from Christians is that while Jews accept Yahweh they do not believe in the God who raised Jesus Christ from the dead.

Polycarpian Anathemas

Indeed, whoever does not acknowledge Jesus Christ to have come in human flesh is Antichrist; whoever does not admit the testimony of the cross is sprung from the devil; whoever twists the Lord's Gospel to suit his own lusts and denies both resurrection and judgment—such a one is the firstborn of Satan. Therefore, let us leave untouched the senseless speculations of the masses and the false doctrines, and turn to the teaching delivered to us in the beginning.

(Philippians 7: based on ACW 6.79)

Commentary: Polpcarp presents, as did Ignatius, the resurrection as a *given,* as a fact of Christian life. Polycarp here appears anything but his former meek self. He seems in fact a trifle vengeful, and has an arsenal of epithets ready for gnostics and docetists. Like Clement and Ignatius he hated heresy. But Polycarp fails to distinguish between the crime and the criminal.

2. THE "LETTER OF BARNABAS"

Introduction

The "Letter of Barnabas" is not a letter and it was not written by the apostle Barnabas. It is a theological instruction coupled with a *Didache*-like recital of moral teaching, describing "two ways" of good and evil. It may be derived from the teaching of the Qumran Dead Sea community which apparently influenced the formation of John the Baptist and possibly John the Evangelist as well. It appears to be the work of an Alexandrian in the first half of the 2nd century—perhaps in 138, and certainly no later. Though the author intends to repudiate Judaism, he is interested in using Old Testament materials, especially "prophecies," as clear arguments for his kind of Christian conclusions.

According to the Promise

And [the Lord], since it was ordained that he should manifest himself in the flesh, endured suffering voluntarily so that he might abolish death and reveal the resurrection from the dead. Thus he was to fulfill the promise made to the fathers and, while preparing a new people for himself, to show, while he

still lived on earth, that having achieved the resurrection, he
would then judge.

("Letter of Barnabas" 5: based on ACW 6.43)

> *Commentary:* We recall that Ignatius had said that the resur-
> rection of Christ was like the other mysteries of Christ and
> that the person of the Lord himself is the real final authority,
> the "official record" on which Christian faith is based. Here
> the author of the "Letter of Barnabas" says something in
> a slightly different way. He sees the resurrection as a necessary
> factor in salvation, and the earthly resurrection of Christ
> as somehow the basis for Christ's judgment. Ignatius pointed
> out that union with God in Christ is the goal of man's risen
> life, and that Christ's resurrection brings with it man's own
> resurrection. "Barnabas" adds that the reason for Christ's
> passion was the abolition of man's death and the revealing
> of man's resurrection according to the promise. The reference
> to the promise is itself important in that we have here a direct
> referral of the promise—made to Abraham and recorded in
> the Jewish scriptures—to resurrection as the ultimate destiny
> of man in Christ, for which the "new people" is a this-worldly
> preparation.

3. THE MARTYRDOM OF POLYCARP

Introduction

Written in the year 156, the "Martyrdom," properly classified
as a letter, fits in well with what we know from other sources
about the character of Polycarp (see introduction to Polycarp
above). The context of the passage below pictures Polycarp, the
pastor, marching naked to his final pulpit. He is seen here as voicing
a prayer marked by a balanced trinitarian doxology and by an
affirmation of Christian confidence in the resurrection.

Risen in the Spirit

When the pyre was prepared . . . he looked up to heaven and
said: "O Lord God, O almighty Father of your beloved and

blessed Son Jesus Christ, through whom we have received the knowledge of you, God of angels and hosts and all creation, and of the whole race of saints who live under your eyes: I bless you, because you have seen fit to grant me this day and this hour, so that I may share among the numbers of the martyrs the cup of your anointed and rise to eternal life both in soul and in body, in virtue of the immortality of the Holy Spirit.

(Martyrdom of Polycarp 14: ACW 6.96-98)

Commentary: Notice the implication here that the cup of suffering the martyr is about to share with Christ is to precede a resurrection to eternal life "in virtue of the immortality of the Holy Spirit." Therefore, the martyr is described as associating himself with the risen Christ with whom, as "eternal and heavenly high priest," Polycarp's "rich and pleasing sacrifice" is about to link him in liturgical offering.

QUESTIONS FOR DISCUSSION

1. Does Polycarp attempt to prove the resurrection of Christ?
2. How does Polycarp express the Pauline conception of God the Father? Why is this significant?
3. Why is the "Letter of Barnabas" a misnomer? What are some of the characteristics of this work?
4. How does the author of the "Letter of Barnabas" use the Old Testament promise made to Abraham in this selection?
5. How does the account of the martyrdom of Polycarp express Christian confidence in the resurrection?

CHAPTER 4

"PROPHECIES"

AND PARALLELS

Prefatory Note

Among the more important of the 2nd-century Greek apologists are Justin Martyr and Theophilus of Antioch. From varying points of view they attempt to establish the credibility of the resurrection through debate and argument with non-Christians.

1. JUSTIN MARTYR

Introduction

Justin was beheaded, perhaps in 165, at the end of a long career of teaching, writing, discussing and arguing with pagans and Jews in defense of Christianity. Our selections are from his so-called *First Apology,* written sometime after 148; the *Dialogue with Trypho,* possibly a stylized version of a discussion between Justin and Rabbi Tarphon mentioned in the Mishna, and written after the *Apology*; and a fragment from a lost treatise *On the Resurrection.* Whether Justin wrote this treatise remains doubtful; but in some ways it reflects ideas in his certainly authentic writings.

"Reasonableness" of Resurrection

If you are not such as you are . . . and someone were to show you human seed and a picture of a man, and assure you

25

that the one could grow into the other, would you believe it before you saw it happening? Undeniably no. In the same way unbelief prevails about the resurrection of the dead because you have never seen an instance of it, but as . . . our teacher, Jesus Christ, said, "The things that are impossible with men are possible with God" [Lk 18:27].

(First Apology 19: based on LCC 1.254)

> *Commentary:* In this famous passage on the Christian doctrine of the resurrection of the dead, Justin makes an interesting comparison, reminiscent of Clement of Rome, in an effort to "convalidate" from nature the comparative "reasonableness" of the resurrection of the dead.

Possessors of the "Mighty Word"

It was said through David the prophet that God the Father of all would take up Christ to heaven after raising him from the dead, and then wait to smite the demons who are his enemies until the number be completed of those whom he foreknows will be good and virtuous. For his sake he has not yet brought about the destruction of the world by fire. The words are these: "The Lord said to my Lord, 'Sit on my right hand until I make your enemies your footstool.' The Lord will send forth the rod of power from Jerusalem, and dominate in the midst of your enemies. The beginning is with you in the day of your power, in the splendor of your holy ones; I have begotten you from the womb before the morning star" [Ps 110: 1-3]. The words, "He will send forth the rod of power from Jerusalem," is a prediction of the mighty Word which the apostles, going forth from Jerusalem, preached everywhere and which, although death is decreed against those who teach or even confess the name of Christ, we everywhere both receive and teach. If you respond to these words with hostility, you can do no more as we said before than to kill us, which will do no harm to us, but will issue in eternal punishment through fire for you and for all who unjustly are enemies [of the Gospel] and do not repent.

(First Apology 45: based on LCC 1.271)

Commentary: Justin adduces, presumably for the enlightenment of his pagan audience, a reference to the psalmist as anticipating prophetically the resurrection and exaltation of Christ. The reference to smiting of demons is not coincidental. Justin likes to remind his partners in dialogue of the bad company they frequent. Like most Christian apologists, Justin sees the human race under a curse due to "malign demons, themselves the product of the union of fallen angels with the daughters of men, [who] swarming everywhere . . . have obsessed men's souls and bodies, infecting them with vice and corruption" (ECD 167). Justin thinks of the risen Lord as obliged to unseat these demons and replace them with saints. Some of Christ's victorious power seems to Justin to be communicated to Christians. But the most important thing for us here is that the apostles, going forth from Jerusalem after the resurrection and exaltation of Christ, are possessors, in virtue of the resurrection and exaltation of Christ, of the "rod of power," and "mighty Word" of the Lord.

Justin and "Those Nasty Rumors"

Note: Unlike the *First Apology,* which was basically Justin's effort to make Christian faith seem reasonable, responsible and possibly attractive to Emperor Antoninus Pius and other pagans, the *Dialogue with Trypho* is designed to show Jews that Christianity has supplanted the Mosaic law, that the former Israel is rejected, and that Christ as God has brought forth a new chosen people, a new Israel.

Now you Jews were well acquainted with these facts in the life of Jonah, and though Christ proclaimed to you that he would give you the sign of Jonah and pleaded with you to repent your sins at least after his resurrection from the dead, and to lament before God as did the Ninevites that your nation and city might not be seized and destroyed as it has been—yet you not only refuse to repent after learning that he arose from the dead, but as I stated, you chose certain men and commissioned them to travel through the whole civilized world and announce: "A godless and lawless sect has been started by an imposter, a certain Jesus of Galilee, whom we nailed to the cross, but whose body, after it was taken down from the cross, was stolen at night from the tomb by his disciples, who now try to deceive men by affirming that he has risen from the dead and has ascended into heaven." And you accuse him of having taught those irreverent, riotous and wicked things of which you everywhere accuse all those who look up and acknowledge him as their Christ, their teacher and the Son of God. . . . Even now, after your city has been seized and your country ravished, you not only refuse to repent but you defiantly curse him and his followers. Yet as far as we Christians are concerned, we do not hate you or the people who believe those nasty rumors you have spread against us. On the contrary, we pray that even now you may reform your ways and find mercy in God the Father of all who is most benevolent and compassionate.

(Dialogue with Trypho 108: based on Williams 223-24)

Commentary: Of interest to us here is Justin's use of Jonah imagery, interpreted in the sense of Matthew 12 as a sign predicting the resurrection. He somewhat naively expects an honest Jew to accept the resurrection as something not only announced in the Old Testament, but announced by Christ under the figure of Jonah and the three days in the whale's belly. It almost seems that Justin's real interest is in loading onto the Jews the responsibility for not only the destruction of Jerusalem as a direct result of their refusal "to repent . . . at least after [Christ's] resurrection from the dead," but also the crime of the Jewish leaders, reported in the New Testament, of bribing the guards to say that the apostles stole Jesus' body from the tomb. The possibility seems to escape him that an intelligent Jew might find some difficulty in the argument about the Jonah story as "prophecy" of the resurrection and the Christian community's version of the Easter story.

Risen in the Flesh

Note: One of the problems dealt with in Christian writing about the resurrection of Christ from the New Testament onward is the matter of bodily resurrection. A posthumous "spiritual" resurrection was widely enough accepted in Greek philosophy to cause little difficulty. In this fragment attributed to Justin we find a reflection of Paul's teaching in 1 Corinthians 15 that Christ's resurrection in the flesh is a guarantee of man's fleshly resurrection.

If the resurrection were only spiritual, he would in raising the dead have had to show the body lying apart by itself and the soul living apart by itself. . . . Why did he rise in the flesh he suffered in, except to show the resurrection of the flesh? And wishing to confirm this, when his disciples did not know whether to believe that he had truly risen in the body and were looking at him and doubting, he said to them, "You do not have faith yet; see that it is I," and he let them handle him and showed them the print of the nails in his hands.

(On the Resurrection—Fragment 9)

Commentary: Here we have a passage very much like that of Ignatius in Smyrnaeans 3, in which the new Testament material on the physical contact with the risen Lord is used to support not the fact of Christ's resurrection (which is simply taken for granted here, as in the two previous passages) but the physical, fleshly character of the resurrection.

2. THEOPHILUS OF ANTIOCH

Introduction

The penchant for using "natural" correlates to establish the reasonableness of the resurrection continues in Theophilus of Antioch. His letter to Autolycus, composed shortly after 180, in effect synthesizes and recapitulates many of the natural metaphors already seen, and adds some original metaphors of his own.

Some Choice Analogies

Then, as to your denying that the dead are raised—for you say, "Show me even one who has been raised from the dead, that seeing I may believe"—first, what great thing is it if you believe when you have seen the thing done? . . . Consider, if you please, the dying of seasons and days and nights, how these also die and rise again. And is there not a resurrection going on of seeds and fruits, and this, too, for the use of men? A seed of wheat, for example . . . when it is cast into the earth, first dies and rots away, then is raised, and becomes a stalk of wheat . . . . Consider the resurrection of the moon . . . the resurrection going on in yourself, even though you are unaware of it. For perhaps you have fallen sick, and lost flesh . . . but when you received again from God mercy and healing, you picked up again in flesh . . . and as you do not know where your flesh went away and disappeared to, so neither do you know whence it grew.   (Theophilus to Autolycus 13: based on ANF 2.92-93)

Commentary: Such generalized descriptions of the resurrection are no doubt primarily intended to prove the possibility of man's resurrection, but they also have, for apologists like Theophilus, a reference to Christ as risen Lord.

QUESTIONS FOR DISCUSSION

1. How does Justin express the "reasonableness" of the resurrection of the dead in his *First Apology?*
2. How does Justin use Old Testament materials in the selection from *First Apology* 45?
3. Why is the human race, according to Justin and other apologists, under a curse?
4. What is Justin's *Dialogue with Trypho* designed to show? How is this done? What are some of the difficulties with this approach?
5. Why is the physical, fleshly character of the resurrection

stressed in some early Christian writing? What is the significance of this emphasis in the fragment from Justin's *On the Resurrection?*

6. What do writers like Theophilus actually prove by using analogies from nature to establish the credibility of resurrection?

CHAPTER 5

EXALTATION

AND GLORIFICATION

Prefatory Note

Important early expositors of the divine attributes of Christ are Melito of Sardis and Irenaeus. Irenaeus, a Greek of Asia Minor, became bishop of Lyons. He attempted the first ordered Christian theology.

1. MELITO OF SARDIS

Introduction

Certainly one of the most brilliant expositors of the glory of the risen Christ is this 2nd-century bishop of Sardis in Lydia. Melito, of special interest for Church historians from Eusebius to Harnack, was described by a contemporary (in language reflecting both Melito's style and his theological viewpoint) as one of the "great luminaries," a man "who lived entirely in the Holy Spirit [and] who lies in Sardis waiting for the visitation from heaven when he will rise from the dead." Melito shared with a few of the greatest fathers a certain Eastern awareness of the numinousness of the risen Christ. In fact, so divine is Melito's Christ and so readily does Melito apply divine and human names to the same person, that Melito's easy language made him suspect of a naive modalism. It also made him popular with that later theological school which insisted that it was the Father who suffered on the cross. Yet obviously much of his writing is perfectly orthodox. His homily is filled with echoes of Christian liturgy and Christian hymnody. The homily begins just after the Exodus story is read from scripture.

Passover and Resurrection

The mystery of the Passover is new and old, eternal and transient, corruptible and incorruptible, mortal and immortal. It is old according to the Law but new according to the Word; transient according to the world, but eternal through grace, corruptible as to the slaughter of the sheep, incorruptible because of the life of the Lord, mortal because of the burial of the Lord, immortal because of his resurrection. . . . In place of the lamb there came a Son, and in place of the sheep a man, and in the man, Christ who contains all things. . . . Born as a Son, led forth as a lamb, sacrificed as a sheep, buried as a man, he rose from the dead as God, being by nature God and man.

(Homily on the Pasch 2-10: Bonner 168-69)

Commentary: In this cadenced opening of the homily—marked by several apparently liturgical sequences, some of which may be a product of Melito's own lyric power—we find the risen Christ celebrated for the newness he brings, the eternity and incorruptibility and immortality through the presence of his Word, his grace, his life and his resurrection. While his passion and death are linked with his lowliness as lamb and sheep, and the burial associated with his manhood, his resurrection is in virtue of his divinity.

"I Lead You Up"

But he arose from the dead to the heights of the heavens: God, who put on man and suffered for the sufferer, was bound for him who was bound, judged for him who was condemned, and buried for him who was buried. And he arose from the dead and cries out to you: "Who is he that struggles against me? Let him stand before me. I freed the condemned; I made the dead live again; I raised him who was buried. Who is he who lifts his voice against me?" He says, "I am the Christ; I am he who put down death and triumphed over the enemy. . . . Come all you families of men . . . and receive remission of sins. For I am your remission. I am the passover of salvation, the one that was sacrificed for you; I am your ransom; I am your light; I am your savior; I am the resurrection; I am your king. I lead you up to the heights of the heavens. I will show you the Father who is from forever; I will raise you up by my right hand." This is he who was made flesh in a virgin, who was hanged from a tree, who was buried in the earth, who rose from the dead and went up to the heights of heaven.

(Homily on the Pasch 100-104: Bonner 180)

Commentary: It is interesting to note the effects of the resurrection as itemized by Melito. The risen Christ freed the condemned, gave life again to the dead and raised the buried. He brings remission of sins to the families of men. He is their ransom, light, savior, resurrection and king. He leads them "up to the heights of the heavens." Melito shows us the many-sidedness of the causal relation between the passion and resurrection of Christ and the redemption and resurrection of man.

2. IRENAEUS

Introduction

Irenaeus was bishop of Lyons in Gaul during the last years of the 2nd century. The first systematic theologian among the fathers and unquestionably the most important theologian of the 2nd century, he was a dedicated anti-gnostic whose theology was focused on the idea of recapitulation (*anakephalaiosis*) drawn from the letters of Paul. Recapitulation means that all creation and all the work of salvation are gathered up, renewed, restored and reordered by the Father in the incarnate Son, the second Adam:

"When he became incarnate and was made man, he recapitulated in himself the long history of man, summing up and giving us salvation in order that we might receive again in Christ Jesus what we had lost in Adam—that is, the image and likeness of God." This quotation is taken from the best and most famous of Irenaeus' extant writings, the treatise usually called *Against Heresies* (3.8). From the same treatise, the texts that follow are among those important to the resurrection.

Restorer of All Things

Now the Church . . . received from the apostles and their disciples its faith in one God, the Father Almighty . . . and in one Christ Jesus, the Son of God, who was made flesh for our salvation, and in the Holy Spirit, who through the prophets proclaimed . . . the birth of a virgin, the suffering, the resurrection from the dead, and the bodily reception into the heavens of the beloved, Christ Jesus our Lord, and his coming from the heavens in the glory of the Father to restore all things, and to raise up all flesh . . . so that every knee may bow . . . to Christ Jesus our Lord and God . . . that he may execute righteous judgment on all. The spiritual powers of wickedness . . . and the godless and wicked . . . among men he will send into the eternal fire. But to the righteous and holy . . . he will by his grace give life incorrupt, and will clothe them with eternal glory.   (Against Heresies 1.10: LCC 1.360)

Commentary: What Irenaeus gives us here is his own brief commentary on the primitive baptismal creeds. While his statement is wholly derived from traditional credal formulae, it has something of his own perspective in it, particularly in its extensive relating of the resurrection and *parousia* of Christ to the behavior of men and angels). Without going into detail on this credal statement, we may point out several relevant features. First, Irenaeus gives considerable attention to the character of the glorified Lord Jesus consequent upon his resurrection and ascension. Second, he sees recapitulation and the raising up of "all flesh" as the work of the glorified Christ—viewed rather more from the perspective of the second coming than from the perspective of his resurrection: Christ returns to get man. Irenaeus differs from some other fathers, who rather see Christ, the "firstborn" from the dead, *leading* men to their resurrection. Third, for Irenaeus the purpose of the resurrection of man lies in the adoration of Christ Jesus as Lord, God, savior and king. Fourth, the confession of Christ, like the judgment of Christ, is accomplished by the destruction of transgressors, angelic and human, and the conferring of life, incorruption and eternal glory upon those who have kept Christ's commandments and abided in his love. In other words, man's resurrection, while it follows upon and is achieved by Christ's glorification, is in Irenaeus very much involved with the good behavior of the candidate.

Creation and Re-Creation

If men think only of the weakness of the flesh, and do not consider the power of him who raises it from the dead, they ignore the might of God. . . . For God fails in power if he does not give life to mortality and bring corruptibility to incorruption. But we ought to infer God's power in all these things from a consideration of our beginning; God took clay from the earth and fashioned man. Now to bring man to being, to make a living and rational creature of bones, muscles, veins and all the rest of man's economy, which as yet did not exist—this was a task far harder, far more incredible, than to restore this creature when he had been created and then redissolved into the earth, having returned to those elements out of which man was first created. If God gave existence, when he so willed, to those who did not exist, much more will he restore those who have come into being to the life which he gave them, if he so wills. The flesh which at the beginning was the subject of God's art will be found capable of receiving and assimilating God's power.

(Against Heresies 5.3: Bettenson 135)

Commentary: We have here a sample of Irenaeus' attempt to prove the reasonableness of the resurrection of the human person. But he argues from within a context of faith. It is assumed that the reader or listener is quite willing to concede the formation of man by God in creation. Like Justin, Irenaeus argues that the making of man in "bones, muscle, veins and all the rest" is in itself incredible. But he assumes something Justin's argument did not assume, that the discussant is willing to accept *God's* making of man. Another assumption of this text, much less explicit, seems to be the paradigm of Christ's resurrection. Without this paradigm Irenaeus would not be able to speak so confidently about "the power of him who raises [the flesh] from the dead."

Death and Restoration

What is restored to life is not something other than that which dies, just as that which is lost is not something different from that which is found. It was a sheep that was lost which the Lord came to find. What then was it which perished? Clearly, it was the substance which lost the breath of life. . . . The Lord came to restore this flesh to life, so that "as in Adam all die," as possessing merely sensual life, we may live "in Christ" [cf. 1 Cor 15:22], as having spiritual life, putting away not the handiwork of God but the lusts of the flesh, and receiving the Holy Spirit.   (Against Heresies 5.12: Bettenson 134-35)

> *Commentary:* What Irenaeus is directly dealing with is the *substantial* identity of the "flesh" which loses life in death and gains life through restoration. Most useful for us in this brief passage is its application of the recapitulation theme to man's resurrection or restoration: the text seems equally applicable to this life and the life beyond. Theologically, what Irenaeus says is unintelligible without the resurrection of Christ. Death comes with Adam; restoration to life comes in Christ. One of the unfortunate features of Irenaeus' theology is that he failed to exploit the theological possibilities of Christ's resurrection in relationship to his theology of recapitulation. This failure may partly be explained by his polemical purpose in writing. The problem is that someone deeply involved in polemical theology may be—precisely to the extent of that involvement—prevented from developing his positive theological views in their fullest, richest implications.

Death to Life

The Lord also declares himself to be the Son of Man, thus renewing in himself that primal man in whom the formation [of
man] by woman began, so that, just as our race went down to
death by a man who was conquered, we might ascend again to
life by a man who overcame; and just as death won the palm of
victory over us by a man, so we might by a man receive the
palm of victory over death.

(Against Heresies 5.21: based on LCC 1.391)

Commentary: In this text we see repeated again, in terms
which clearly reflect a consideration of the risen Christ as
the cause of man's passage from death to life, Irenaeus' familiar
doctrine of Christ as the new Adam.

Movement toward Vision

The apostle has proclaimed that "creation shall be liberated
from the bondage of corruption and obtain the glorious liberty
of the sons of God" [Rom 8:21]. And in all and through all the
same God the Father is displayed, who fashioned man and
promised to the fathers the inheritance of the earth, and "led
out that inheritance" in the resurrection of the righteous, and
fulfills his promises in the kingdom of his Son, afterward be-
stowing, with fatherly love, things "which eye has not seen,
nor ear heard, nor the heart of man conceived" [1 Cor 2:9].

(Against Heresies 5.36: Bettenson 140)

Commentary: Here we see Irenaeus' idea that fullness of
possession of the unseen is something gradually attained.
Three basic stages are pretty clearly distinguished. First, there
is the present life which involves "the bondage of corruption";
second, there is the inheritance which is "led out" in the resurrection of the just, in the kingdom of the Son in which the
promises are fulfilled; third, "afterward" there is the bestowal
in love of final, everlasting vision. For Irenaeus the glorifi-

cation of creation comes at the second stage; it seems to be an intermediate situation.

QUESTIONS FOR DISCUSSION

1. What awareness did Melito of Sardis share with some of the greatest fathers? What heresy was Melito suspected of and why?
2. In the selection from the *Homily on the Pasch 100-104,* what are some of the effects of Christ's resurrection listed by Melito?
3. What is meant by recapitulation in the writings of Irenaeus of Lyons? From where is this concept drawn?
4. How does Irenaeus elaborate his own point of view in the credal passage given?
5. How does Irenaeus argue the reasonableness of the resurrection? What assumptions are present in Irenaeus which are not found in Justin?
6. How can you explain Irenaeus' failure to develop the theological possibilities of Christ's resurrection?
7. Explain Irenaeus' idea of the three basic stages of redemption. Where does the glorification of creation fit in?

CHAPTER 6
TRANSFORMATION
THROUGH UNION

Introduction

Origen (d. 255), director of the famous Alexandrian catechetical school, was in many ways the greatest, though not the most orthodox, early Christian writer. His philosophical Platonism and religious mysticism were combined in his theory of the incarnation. In the pre-existent world of spiritual beings, one soul clung with burning love to the Logos—the Word—while all others were unfaithful. This one fervently devoted soul became the soul of the human Christ. At the resurrection Christ's humanity becomes deified and his body takes on a special "spiritual" quality. Through his resurrection and exaltation, the savior seems to become gradually disembodied. He who "was a man, now no longer is one." So essentially Christ's resurrection was the first step in the full divinization of his human nature, which in glory becomes all too fully fused into the Word. Christ in his passion and resurrection overthrows once and for all the powers of darkness, the demonic forces.

Transformation in Christ

With a view to giving us the blessings of the firstborn, he himself becomes "firstborn from the dead," that he himself might have the primacy in everything, and may take up us, who believe in his resurrection, for his first fruits . . . if, indeed, we

41

keep firm hold on the grace of these blessings to the end, aided by the mercy of our Lord Jesus Christ himself.

(Homily on Numbers [3:4]: Drewery 132)

> *Commentary:* Origen allegorizes his Old Testament source to make it foreshadow Colossians 1, in which Paul says that Christ "is the beginning, the firstborn from the dead. . . . God was pleased . . . through him to reconcile to himself all things" [Col 1:18-20]. The pattern Origen seems to be working out here is this: Christ is firstborn from the dead; Christians—i.e., those "who believe in his resurrection"—are the first harvest, the first taken up into exaltation by the firstborn; the whole of creation (perhaps even the devil) will, as we learn from other sources in Origen, be taken up in the final restoration. In any event Christ's resurrection is clearly the paradigm for the transformation and exaltation of man through union with the Logos.

Images of the Resurrection

So have the things delivered through our Lord Jesus Christ himself been set in true gold and in solid silver. . . . For when he has laid him down and slept "as a lion and as a lion's whelp" [cf. Gen 49:9], and afterward the Father has aroused him, and he has risen from the dead, if then there be such as have been made conformable to his resurrection, they will continue no longer in the likeness of gold, that is, in the pursuit of bodily things, but will receive the true gold from him.

(Commentary on the Song of Songs [2.8]: ACW 26.153-55)

> *Commentary:* Evoking the Genesis account of Jacob's blessing on Judah, Origen pictures the buried Lord as a sleeping lion. Aroused by the Father in the resurrection, the Lord Jesus is instrumental in making those who (in this life) "have been made conformable to his resurrection" fully authentic persons. It appears that for Origen conformity to Christ's resurrection makes people "like gold" in the present existence, and that their quality as "true gold" awaits a further "spiritualization" and fuller identification with the Lord.

The Church Must Rise

"Arise; come, my neighbor, my fair one, my dove; for lo, the winter is past; the rain is gone and has departed to itself; the flowers have appeared on the earth. . . ." [cf. Song 2:10-12]

We can say that it is a sort of prophecy given to the Church, to call her to the promised blessings of the future. She is told to "arise," as though the consummation of the age were already reached and the time of resurrection come. And, because this word of command forthwith seals the work of resurrection, she is invited into the kingdom, as being now, by virtue of the resurrection, brighter and more splendid.

(Commentary on the Song of Songs [3.14]:
ACW 26.239, 245)

Commentary: The "beloved" of the Song of Songs is here allegorically interpreted as anticipating the Church. The Church then is commanded to rise in greater brightness and splendor, as though the consummation had come and in her resurrection the Church were ready to be invited into the kingdom. The time of "consummation" Origen has in mind is perhaps the "general resurrection." But the important feature here is that the Church as well as the individual is seen as commanded to arise, to move toward the promised blessings of the future.

Christ Risen and Reigning

For so long as Christ "had not been raised from the dead, the first fruits of them that are asleep" [cf. 1 Cor 15:20], and those who became conformed to his death and resurrection had not been raised along with him, the city of God was sought for below, and the temple, and the purifications, and the rest; but when this took place, no longer were the things below sought for, but the things above; and, in order that these might be set up, it was necessary that he should go into the Jerusalem below, and there suffer many things from the elders and the chief priests and scribes of the people, in order that he might be glorified by the heavenly elders who could receive his bounties, and by diviner high priests who are ordained under the one high priest, and that he might be glorified by the scribes of the people who are occupied with letters "not written with ink" [cf. 2 Cor 3:3] but made clear by the Spirit of the living God, and might be killed in the Jerusalem below, and, having risen from the dead, might reign in Mount Zion and the city of the living God —the heavenly Jerusalem. But on the third day he rose from the dead, in order that having delivered them from the wicked one and his son, in whom was falsehood and unrighteousness and war and everything opposed to that which Christ is, and also from the profane spirit who transforms himself into the Holy Spirit, he might gain for those who had been delivered the right to be baptized in spirit and soul and body, into the name of the Father and the Son and the Holy Spirit, who represent the three days eternally present at the same time to those who by means of them are sons of light.

(Commentary on Matthew [20]: based on ANF 9.462)

Commentary: Christ's resurrection was antecedently necessary for the resurrection of those "conformed to his death and resurrection." Under the old dispensation the city or kingdom of God was sought for in human religious ritual. As Origen seems to see it, "the Jerusalem below" was (possibly by way of contrast) the "necessary" locus for Christ's suffering and death, the needed earthly preparation for his risen reign in the heavenly kingdom, "the city of the living God—the heavenly Jerusalem." But Origen moves into freewheeling allegory in the identification of the Father, Son and Holy Spirit with the "three days." These in turn he may be thinking of in the liturgical context of the Easter vigil (note the references to baptism and the use of the metaphor of light).

Resurrection of the Church

Now both of these things, the temple and the body of Jesus, appear to me, in one interpretation at least, to be types of the

Church, and to signify that it is built of living stones, a spiritual house for a holy priesthood, built on the foundation of the apostles and prophets, Christ Jesus being the chief cornerstone; and it is, therefore, called a temple. And thus the resurrection of the savior from the passion of the cross contains the mystery of the resurrection of the whole body of Christ. But as that material body of Jesus was sacrificed for Christ, and was buried, and was afterward raised, so the whole body of Christ's saints is crucified along with him, and now lives no longer; for each of them, like Paul, glories in nothing but the cross of our Lord Jesus Christ, through which he is crucified to the world, and the world to him. Not only, therefore, is it crucified with Christ, and crucified to the world; it is also buried with Christ, for we were buried with Christ, Paul says [cf. Rom 6:4]. And then he says, as if enjoying some earnest of the resurrection, "We rose with him," because he walks in a certain newness of life, though not yet risen in that blessed and perfect resurrection which is hoped for.

(Commentary on John [20]: based on ANF 9.400-01)

Commentary: We saw, in the commentary on the Song of Songs (3:14), Origen's view of the Church as in her risen state bright and splendid, the "beloved" of Christ. Here Origen clearly relates the resurrection of the Church as the "body of Christ" to the resurrection of the savior. The "mystery of the resurrection of the whole body of Christ" is contained within the resurrection of the savior. The Church, mystically crucified and buried with Christ, has prospectively risen with him. . . . On the supposition that Origen is trying to describe the Church of his era in terms of the mystery of Christ, it seems that he sees her as either crucified or buried. In any case, the Church, the body of Christ, "the whole body of Christ's saints," lives in hope of resurrection.

A Progressive Resurrection

But they are destroyed to be raised again by Jesus, not on the third day, if we attend to the exact words before us, but "in three days." For the rising again of the temple takes place on the first day after it has been destroyed and on the second day, and its resurrection is accomplished in all the three days. Hence a resurrection both has been and is to be, if indeed we were buried with Christ and rose with him. And since the word, "We rose with him," does not cover the whole of the resurrection, "in Christ shall all be made alive. But in his own order: Christ the first fruits, at his coming those who belong to Christ, then the end" [1 Cor 15:22-25]. It belongs to the resurrection that one should be on the first day in the paradise of God, and it belongs to the resurrection when Jesus appears and says, "Touch me not, for I am not yet ascended to my Father" [Jn 20: 17]. But the perfection of the resurrection was when he came to the Father.   (Commentary on John [21]: based on ANF 9.402)

> *Commentary:* Origen here sees the resurrection of the "holy priesthood . . . the whole body of Christ's saints" as a progressive event. Moreover, resurrection is something both accomplished in men in the past—something already realized —and something to be accomplished in the future. The realized resurrection of man is epitomized in the parascriptural statement, "We rose with him." The future resurrection—the "not yet" of contemporary theological usage—is epitomized in the scriptural statement, "In Christ shall all be made alive." Even Christ's resurrection is for Origen something gradually achieved, gradually realized in him. At first it is imperfect—the presence of Christ "in the paradise of God" but as one who has not yet ascended. The perfection of Christ's resurrection is in his exaltation, his glorification, after he comes to the Father.

The Risen Christ as Energizing Light

Now he is called the light of men and the true light and the light of the world because he brightens and irradiates . . . all reasonable beings. And similarly it is from and because of the energy with which he causes the old deadness to be put aside, and causes life *par excellence* to be put on—so that those who have truly received him rise again from the dead—that he is called the resurrection. And this he does not only at the moment at which a man says, "We are buried with Christ through baptism and have risen again with him" [cf. Rom 6:4], but rather when a man, having laid off all about him that belongs to death, walks in the newness of life which belongs to him the Son, while here. We always "carry about in our body the dying of the Lord Jesus," and thus we reap the vast advantage, "that the life of the Lord Jesus might be made manifest in our bodies" [2 Cor 4:10].

(Commentary on John [25]: based on ANF 9.312)

Commentary: Christ, seen by Origen as light in his illumination of the human spirit, is called the resurrection because of the "energy" he brings to bear on the putting aside of former deadness and putting on of life in its highest sense. Christ's "energy" as risen is present to a person not so much at his baptismal burial and rising, but at his consistent later walking in "newness of life." We notice Origen's stress on the earthly Christ as conferring resurrection, in view of what he was "while here"—i.e., before the ascension. What the final statement may mean is that human suffering, bodily-based suffering, viewed as a dying of the Lord Jesus within man, brings the "vast advantage" of manifesting in human infirmity the life of the Lord Jesus.

Victorious Servant

What . . . great things must be said of the lamb of God, who was sacrificed for this very reason, that he might take away the sin not of a few but of the whole world, for the sake of which also he suffered? . . . And having by his passion destroyed his enemies, he who is strong in battle and a mighty Lord required after his mighty deeds a purification which could only be given him by his Father alone; and this is why he forbids Mary to touch him, saying, "Touch me not, for I am not yet ascended to my Father. . . ." [Jn 20:17]. And when he comes, loaded with victory and with trophies, with his body which has risen from the dead . . . then there are certain powers which say,

"Who is this that comes from Edom, in crimson garments from Bozrah, he who is beautiful?" [cf. Is 63:1]. Then those who escort him say to those that are upon the heavenly gates, "Lift up your gates, you rulers, and be you lifted up, you everlasting doors, and the king of glory shall come in." But they ask again, seeing as it were, his right hand red with blood and his whole person covered with the marks of his valor, "Why are your garments red, and your clothes like the treading of the full wine vat when it is trodden?" [cf. Is 63:2]. And to this he answers, "I have crushed them" [Is 63:3]. For when he had taken up our infirmities and carried our diseases, and had borne the sin of the whole world, and had conferred blessings on so many, then, perhaps, he received that baptism which is greater than any that could be conceived among men, and of which I think he speaks when he says, "I have a baptism to be baptized with, and how am I straitened till it be accomplished" [Lk 12: 50].   (Commentary on John [37]: based on ANF 9.378-79)

Commentary: Here we have an example of the richly liturgical use of Deutero-Isaian servant imagery—in fact, "suffering servant" imagery—in a context of victory and triumph. The resurrection eliminates and transfigures the Christ of the passion. He appears as mighty Lord, loaded with victory and trophies; he comes in splendor as king of glory. Along a different line, we notice again Origen's idea of a progressive resurrection of Christ, the final stage of which requires "a purification which could be given him by his Father alone." Christ must move beyond his tangible condition as risen Lord on earth in order to attain the perfection of the resurrection.

Pattern of Regeneration

Just as through having Adam as the first example, the head, of our natural mode of birth, we are all said to have in this re-spect one body, even so do we register Christ as our head through the divine regeneration of his death and resurrection which has become a pattern for us.

(Commentary on John, fragment 140: based on Drewery 132)

Commentary: Our common "Adamite" origin gives us one body under the headship of Adam. Likewise, Christ is the head of the new, regenerated body of mankind. He is the firstborn exemplar of this new, divine rebirth in his death and resurrection.

The God Who Raised Jesus

Note: Here Origen is commenting on Romans 4:23-25. The question he is asking is why Paul gives the Christian as the object of his faith the God who raised Christ from the dead rather than, for example, the God who created heaven and earth. Origen's answer is that the former designation glorifies God the Father more than the latter one.

For the latter meant the making of what did not exist, the former the redeeming of what had perished. . . . The latter . . . was achieved by a mere fiat, the former by suffering. Now the pattern and image of this . . . mystery had come beforehand in the faith of Abraham. For he had believed, when he was ordered to sacrifice his only son, that God was able to raise him even from the dead; he had also believed that the transaction then set afoot did not only apply to Isaac, but that it was sacramental, and that its full meaning was reserved for that descendant of his who is Christ. It was then . . . with joy that he offered his only son, because he saw therein not the death of his issue, but the restoration of the world, the renewal of the whole creation, reestablished through the resurrection of the Lord: And this was why the Lord said of him, "Your father Abraham rejoiced to see my day. . . ." [Jn 8:56].

Commentary: Origen treats Abraham as a kind of Christian visionary, whose sacrifice of his son Isaac more than made sense because God could raise Isaac from the dead, and because in the offering of Isaac lay the beginnings of a "sacramental transaction" whose ultimate result was to be restoration, renewal and reestablishment in Christ's resurrection of the world and the whole creation. Most important here is the power of Origen's vision of the meaning of the resurrection. Origen then asks another question: Why does Paul make special mention, in speaking of Christian faith, of the resurrection of Christ? There are many other titles of Christ Paul could have used— Wisdom, Virtue, Word, Truth and Light. Origen refers to Ephesians 2:6 which speaks of the Father as having "raised us up with Christ, and made us sit with him in the heavenly places in Christ Jesus." Origen then goes on:

If you believe that Christ has risen from the dead, you must believe also that you yourselves have likewise risen with him; and if you believe that he is seated at the right hand of the Father in heaven, you must also believe that you yourselves are situated no longer in the earthly but the heavenly scene; and if you believe yourselves dead with Christ, you must believe that you will also live with him; and if you believe that Christ is dead to sin and lives to God, you too must be dead to sin and alive to God. . . . This is because the man who [sets his mind on things above] shows his belief in him who raised up Jesus . . . from the dead, and for this man faith is truly counted for righteousness. . . . In the same way . . . believers in Christ who do not "put off the old man with his unrighteous practices" [Col 3:9] cannot have their faith counted for righteousness . . . showing that [our sins] for which Christ was betrayed ought to be abhorred and cast off by us also. . . . For if we retain any further kinship with sin . . . we show that we think the death of Christ Jesus of no account, because we embrace . . . the things that he subdued and conquered.

The apostle, putting this all together, called it the "clothing of the old man" . . . which he urges those to cast off who believe in him who raised . . . Jesus from the dead, so that, casting off the clothing of unrighteousness, they may put on our Lord Jesus, who is the true clothing of righteousness—that their lives may be worthy of their belief, and thus their faith may count for righteousness. . . . And if we have risen with Christ who is righteousness, and walk in newness of life, and live according to righteousness, Christ has risen for us, that we might be justified . . . who have undertaken a new life on the model of his resurrection. . . .

(Commentary on Romans [4:7]: based on Drewery 133-35)

Commentary: Origen's answer to the question, "Why the emphasis on Christ's resurrection?" seems to be the significance of that resurrection for man. Origen insists that the baptismal dying, burial and rising with Christ was not the whole story. Here he repeatedly emphasizes the need to walk in righteousness or justice—to be like Christ, dead to sin, alive to God. The resurrection challenges man to show his belief in the Father as the agent of Christ's resurrection by living that resurrection—setting his mind on "things above," putting off the old man of sin, the "clothing" of sin, that he may "put on our Lord Jesus."

Beyond Suffering to Life

Note: One of the reasons for Origen's prolific output—his treatises numbered at least 2,000, and possibly as many as 6,000, though the overwhelming majority of these are lost—was a wealthy friend named Ambrose. A convert from Valentinian gnosticism, he supplied Origen with batteries of stenographers, including some "young girls," to take down his lecture notes in relays. About the year 178, Celsus, a pagan philosopher who had studied very thoroughly the Christian religion, attacked it in his *True Discourse.* Celsus' purpose was to win over Christians to paganism. About 246 (68 years afterward), Origen's friend Ambrose read Celsus' *True Discourse* and asked Origen (by then over 60 years old) to refute it. Origen could not refuse his friend. Though he thought defensive apologetics of little value, Origen undertook the work, protesting to Ambrose that "the apologia which you ask me to write can only weaken this apologia in action—the power of Jesus which is evident to every man who is not insensible. But alas, in order not to seem to refuse your request, I have tried my best to reply to each of Celsus' attacks, although in my opinion no believer could be shaken by his statements" [*Against Celsus:* Pref. 3].

He rose from the dead and so utterly convinced his disciples of the truth of his resurrection that they show to all men through their sufferings that their attention is focused on life everlasting and on the resurrection which has been exemplified to them in word and deed. And so they can mock at all the hardships of this life.   (Against Celsus 2.77: Drewery 132)

Commentary: Origen seems to see the conviction of the resurrection of Christ as influencing Christians to look beyond their sufferings to "life everlasting and the resurrection." He seems to be echoing Paul's remark about Christ despising the pain in view of "the joy set before him" when he speaks of the disciples of Christ as able to "mock at all the hardships of this life."

The Dynamic Christ

How could a phantom which—in [Celsus'] words—"crept stealthily" on those who saw it to deceive them, even after the moment of vision have had such a great effect on them as to convert so many souls and bring home to them the conviction that they ought to do everything with a view to satisfying God because they will be judged by him? And how could a so-called "phantom" drive out demons and bring about all the other tremendous results? Nor has he been limited to one place like the anthropomorphic gods of Celsus, but ranges the world, gathering and attracting by his divinity any whom he finds giving themselves to the search for the good life.

(Against Celsus 7.35: Drewery 133)

Commentary: Celsus had described the risen Jesus as a "phantom." Origen, confronted by an objection (a not entirely insupportable objection if we recall the way the evangelists sometimes told their story), does in any case argue very clearly and powerfully against applying the term "phantom" to the risen Jesus. For Origen the risen Jesus is a compelling, forceful personality who transcends spatial limits in his world-ranging divine influence upon men. Christ here seems to be seen as influencing not Christians only, but "any whom he finds giving themselves to the search for the good life."

What makes his answer to Celsus' objection especially interesting is that Origen's writings portray the risen human Christ and his body as being so ethereal and spiritual that one not sharing Origen's sophisicated perspective might readily describe Origen's human Christ as a "phantom." But here, against Celsus' stealthy, ineffectual ghost, Origen effectively pits his vision of a transcendent, dynamic, divine Lord, filling the world with his presence and influence, "tremendous" in the "results" he achieves through his disciples in good people everywhere.

QUESTIONS FOR DISCUSSION

1. Give a brief sketch of Origen's theory of the incarnation. What is the significance of Christ's passion and resurrection in Origen's theory? What finally happens to mankind and creation?

2. How does Origen convey his idea that both the individual and the Church are called to risen life *now?* Give examples.

3. According to Origen, is the "energy" of the risen Christ present to a person primarily at his baptism? Explain.

4. How does Origen use the Deutero-Isaian image of the servant? Why does he use an imagery of suffering in a context of victory and triumph? Discuss.

5. Explain Origen's vision of the meaning of the resurrection. What does he emphasize? How does he use Old Testament material? How does Origen conceive of the risen Jesus?

CHAPTER 7

EUCHARIST

AND HOLY SPIRIT

Prefatory Note

With Hippolytus and Novatian we move from the Greek to the Roman world of the 2nd and 3rd centuries. Since Hippolytus wrote in Greek, he is a kind of natural link between the great early Christian writers and the theological tradition of the West; Novatian, part heretic but mostly quite orthodox (his ecclesiastical ambitions seem to be what really got him into trouble), was the first Roman theologian to publish in Latin.

1. HIPPOLYTUS

Introduction

Hippolytus, a Roman martyred in 235, reveals in his writings a background and outlook strongly suggestive of his Eastern origins. Theologically, Hippolytus reaffirms Irenaeus' idea of the recapitulation of all things in Christ. From the apologists he derived the idea that redemption is mostly achieved by *knowledge* of God as mediated by the Lord. The Word is contained in nature, history, the law and the prophets, and finally made manifest in the Gospel.

Christ as Judge

But since the savior was the beginning of the resurrection of all men, it was proper that the Lord alone should rise from the dead, by whom, too, the judgment is to enter for the whole world, that they who have wrestled worthily may be also crowned worthily by the illustrious arbiter—by him who himself first finished the course and was received into the heavens and seated at the right hand of God the Father, and who is to be manifested again at the end of the world as judge.

(Treatise on Christ and Antichrist 46: based on ANF 5.213)

> *Commentary:* This treatise, written about the year 200, shows Hippolytus' millenarian concern with judgment. Hippolytus sees the resurrection of Christ as important, not simply as "the beginning of the resurrection of all men," but as establishing Christ's power as judge.

The Eucharist as Revelation

And when he gave himself over to voluntary suffering, so as to destroy death and to break the bonds of the devil . . . and to illuminate the righteous . . . and to reveal the resurrection, he took bread, gave thanks, and said: "Take, eat, this is my body which is broken for you." In the same manner also the cup, and said: "This is my blood which is poured out for you. As often as you do this, you keep my memory."

When we remember his death and his resurrection in this way, we bring to you the bread and the cup, and give thanks to you, because you have thought us worthy to stand before you and to serve you as priests.

(Apostolic Tradition: based on Dix 4)

> *Commentary:* Except for the *Didache,* the most important source for primitive Church orders and liturgy is Hippolytus' *Apostolic Tradition.* Here we find described the liturgy of Rome—probably as performed during the latter half of the 2nd century, since Hippolytus wanted to record only the forms and rites established through long usage. The material above is taken from what Hippolytus presents as an exemplar for the canon in the Mass liturgy. His canon is more richly Christo-

logical than present-day Roman canons. Notice that Hippolytus says that the eucharist has as its purpose "to *reveal* the resurrection." It is also a *memorial* of Christ's death and resurrection. Here we find the theme prominent in several other fathers —the close association between the resurrection and the eucharist.

2. NOVATIAN

Introduction

Hippolytus has in his own theology the idea of a progressively developing Word whose generation was a free act like creation. Novatian (d. ca. 257) had a similar Word-theology. He makes Christ the Son and servant of the Father, subordinate to the Father. Probably a Christian Stoic, Novatian and his followers took a rigorist, Catharistic (or Puritan) attitude toward those who had lapsed from the Church during persecution. The Novatians denied that post-baptismal sins could be forgiven.

Imperishable Flesh

In fact, we reject every other Christ devised by heretics with a fictional body of any kind whatever. The birth of the Lord, equally with his death, puts them all out of the question. "The Word," says John, "became flesh and dwelt among us" [Jn 1:14]; as the Word took on flesh, Christ must have had a human body. And the blood flowed from his hands and feet, and even from his side, in proof that he, dying . . . shared our human body, and the wounds in that same body proved that he was raised in the substance of the very body in which he died. This restoration, in his resurrection, of the very body which he derived from us men shows us the conditions of our resurrection. In Christ's rising from the dead in the substance of his body, as the norm of all, the law of resurrection is laid down. True, it is written that "flesh and blood cannot inherit the kingdom of God" [1 Cor 15:50], but it is not that the substance of our flesh is condemned. This was fashioned by the hands of God, so as not to perish. It is only the guilt of the flesh that is censured . . . man's rash and willful rebellion against the requirements of the divine law. But when this guilt has been taken away in baptism, and in the dissolution brought about by death, then the deathfulness of sin is put away, and the flesh is recalled to a state of innocence, and so restored to salvation.

Commentary: Here Novatian attacks a docetist view—that Christ's resurrection body was fictional. In his resurrection Christ had "the substance of the very body in which he died" restored to him. In this respect, Christ's resurrection formed a paradigm of man's. The "substance of our flesh" is not condemned but "recalled to a state of innocence." What is condemned in man and destroyed or "censured" is guilt, "the deathfulness of sin."

The Spirit Given in the Resurrection

So it is one and the same Spirit who is in the prophets and in the apostles; only that he is in the prophets to meet a particular situation, but in the apostles at all times. In other words, he is not in the prophets so as to be in them always, but is in the apostles so as to abide in them always; he is in the prophets as doled out in moderation, but in the apostles as poured forth in his entirety; he is in the prophets as given sparingly, but in the apostles as given generously. And yet [the Spirit] is not given before the resurrection of the Lord, but bestowed through the resurrection of Christ.

Commentary: The most important observation to be made here is that Novatian holds, as other fathers do, that the Holy Spirit is given to men not at Pentecost but in the event of the resurrection. Not that the Spirit was not also given earlier. But here the Spirit is poured forth abundantly, is given in "his entirety."

QUESTIONS FOR DISCUSSION

1. In what ways is Hippolytus a link between the tradition of the East and West?
2. What relationship between the resurrection and the eucharist is expressed in Hippolytus' *Apostolic Tradition?* What does this indicate about the early Church?
3. Why did Novatian stress that in his resurrection Christ had "the substance of the very body in which he died"? Explain.
4. In Novatian's view, when was the Holy Spirit given to man?

CHAPTER 8

VENGEANCE

AND VICTORY

Prefatory Note

Quasten observes that, "although the Church of Africa had a relatively late beginning, her contribution to early Christian literature is far greater than Rome's [Quasten 2.243]. Two significant early thinkers of this Church, Tertullian and Cyprian, have interesting things to say about the resurrection.

1. TERTULLIAN

Introduction

Tertullian, who died about 220, is in a number of ways the great-grandfather of certain mischievous tendencies in Western (as distinguished from Eastern) theology. His outlook was juridical; he emphasized less the redemption accomplished by Christ and more the theme of the Christian fighting against sin and practicing "the virtues." He had narrow moral notions—and they led him into Montanism, in which heretical sect he remained until his death. His conception of the "resurrection of the flesh" was crude and unscriptural, and unlike most Eastern theologies, it emphasized a literal resurrection of the human body in which none of the constituents will be lost, "not even a hair or an eye or a tooth." Ramsey notes: "For centuries, many Christians have had a mental picture of material particles of dead bodies reassembled, and of the bodies rising from their graves at the last day." Though this view is strongly supported by Tertullian and many of the Latin and Reformation writers who followed him, it "is a belief which the creed does not compel and which Paul's teaching does not encourage" (Ramsey 111). Tertullian's theory that bad deeds demand satisfaction introduced a legalistic interpretation of the passion, death and resurrection of Christ as making satisfaction for man's sins, an idea prevalent since then in Latin theology.

A Vindictive Christ

And yet, nailed upon the cross, he exhibited many notable signs by which his death was distinguished from all others . . . . Then, when his body was taken down from the cross and placed in a sepulchre, the Jews in their eager watchfulness surrounded it with a large military guard, lest, as he had predicted his resurrection from the dead on the third day, his disciples might remove by stealth his body and deceive even the incredulous. But behold, on the third day there was a sudden shock of earthquake, and the stone which sealed the sepulchre was rolled away, and the guard fled off in terror. Without a single disciple near, the grave was found empty of all but the clothes of the buried one. But nevertheless, the leaders of the Jews, whom it most concerned both to spread abroad a lie and to keep back from the faith a people tributary and submissive to them, gave it out that the body of Christ had been stolen by his followers. For the Lord, you see, did not go forth into the public gaze, lest the wicked should be delivered from their error; that faith also, destined to a great reward, might hold its ground in difficulty.

(Apology 221: based on ANF 2.35)

Commentary: This text is taken from Tertullian's most important work. Consistent with its title, it makes an apologetic defense of the resurrection. This is done through recapitulation of prominent parts of the Gospel narrative. And the Lord is represented as somewhat vindictive, for he avoided the general public "lest the wicked should be delivered from their error."

Man in Christ Made Alive in the Flesh

Moreover, as resurrection accrues to what is dead, and dead is a term applicable only to a body, therefore the body alone has a resurrection incidental to it. So again the word "resurrection" (or "rising again"), embraces only that which has fallen down, because it is by rising *again*, in consequence of its having fallen down, that it is said to have rerisen. . . . For to the body it was said: "Dust you are and unto dust you shall return" [Gen 3:19]. Since by man came death, by man came also the resurrection. Here in the word "man," who consists of bodily substance as we have often shown already, is presented to me the body of Christ. But if we are all made alive in Christ in the way we die in Adam, it follows of necessity that we are made alive in Christ as a bodily substance, since we died in Adam as a bodily substance. The similarity, indeed, is not complete unless our survival in Christ concurs in identity of substance with our mortality in Adam. . . . The resurrection of the body will receive all the better proof, in proportion as I shall succeed in showing that Christ belongs to that God who is believed to have provided this resurrection of the flesh in his dispensation. When he says, "For he must reign till he has put all enemies under his feet" [cf. 1 Cor 15:25], we can see at once from this statement that he speaks of a God of vengeance.

(Against Marcion 5.9: based on ANF 3.447-48)

Commentary: Tertullian here defends the bodily resurrection. It is precisely the body that has fallen down in death which will "rerise." Men who have died in Adam have died in their "bodily substance"; so that is the way they are made alive in Christ. Here also we see Tertullian explicitly putting forward his "God of vengeance." Christ's reign through the promise of his Father as the God of vengeance is a vindictive reign.

Literalistic View of Man's Resurrection

The Lord explains to us the meaning of the thing when he says: "I came not to do my own will, but the Father's, who has sent me" [Jn 6:38]. What, I ask, is that will? "That of all which he has given me I should lose nothing, but should raise it up again on the last day" [Jn 6:39]. Now, what had Christ received of the Father but that which he had himself put on? Man, of course, in his texture of body and soul. Therefore, neither of those parts which he has received will he allow to perish . . . not the least fraction of either.

(On the Resurrection of the Flesh 34: based on ANF 3.570)

> *Commentary:* Here Tertullian says that no part of man, "not the least fraction" of body or soul, will perish. This is one statement of Tertullian's crudely literalistic view of the resurrection of the flesh.

2. CYPRIAN OF CARTHAGE

Introduction

Cyprian, born in Africa early in the 3rd century, died there a martyr in 258. His polished style made him one of the most widely read fathers from his time until the Middle Ages. His eucharistic sacrifice consists in the offering by Christians of the sacrifice which the Lord himself offered. This kind of thinking has tended to obscure the meaning of the eucharist as a sign and revelation of the risen Christ.

Assurance of Victory

Finally the apostle Paul reproaches, rebukes and blames any who are in sorrow at the departure of their friends. "I would not," says he, "have you ignorant, brethren, concerning those who are asleep, that you may not grieve as others do who have no hope. For since we believe that Jesus died and rose again, even so, through Jesus, God will bring with him those who have fallen asleep" [1 Thess 4:13]. He says that those who have sorrow in the departure of their friends have no hope. But we who live in hope, and believe in God, and trust that Christ suffered for us and rose again, abiding in Christ and through him and in him rising again, why are we ourselves unwilling to depart hence from this life? Or why do we bewail and grieve for our friends when they depart as if they were lost, when Christ himself, our Lord and God, encourages us and says, "I am the resurrection and the life. He who believes in me, though he die, yet shall he live, and whoever lives and believes in me shall never die" [Jn 11:25]? If we believe in Christ, let us have faith in his work and promises; and since we shall not die eternally, let us come with glad assurance to Christ, with whom we are both to conquer and to reign forever.

(Treatise on Mortality 21: based on ANF 5.474)

Commentary: This treatise, usually referred to as "On Mortality," was written in the wake of persecution and plague in an effort to explain what death means for the Christian. What Cyprian stresses here is that the Christian has a different view of death because he lives in hope of resurrection in Christ. A Christian's resurrection—which is seen here, as in Tertullian, in terms only of the afterlife—involves a victory like that of Christ in and with whom Christians both conquer and reign forever. In Cyprian's view, as we know from other sources, no such victory awaits non-Christians. Triumphant immortality and everlasting happiness are denied those who are outside the Church [cf. Cyprian's treatise *On The Unity of the Church*].

QUESTIONS FOR DISCUSSION

1. The author says Tertullian is the "great-grandfather" of certain tendencies in Western theology. What are some examples?
2. How should the Christian view death, according to Cyprian of Carthage? Does Cyprian see man's resurrection in terms of the present life?

CHAPTER 9

INCORRUPTION
AND SOLIDARITY

Prefatory Note

Moving back to the world of Greek thought, we encounter two thinkers known for their orthodoxy. The first, Methodius, represents an Aristotelian reaction against Origen's brilliantly Platonizing theology. The second, Athanasius, is famous in Christian history not only as anti-Arian, but as an original Christian thinker who tackles theological problems with a high degree of intelligence, imagination and marked independence of judgment.

1. METHODIUS

Introduction

Methodius (d. 311) was probably a bishop of Philippi in Macedonia during the second half of the 3rd century. An important adversary of Origen, he attacked Origen's teaching on the pre-existence of the soul and tried to refute Origen's spiritualistic interpretation of resurrection. He defends the identity of the earthly body with the resurrection body and, in his *Discourse on the Resurrection*, sees Christ's resurrection as the prototype and cause of man's.

Flesh Raised to Incorruption

"As we have borne the image of the earthly, we shall also bear the image of the heavenly" [cf. 1 Cor 15:49]. For the

67

image of the earthly which we have borne is this: "Dust you are, and unto dust you shall return" [Gen 3:19]. But the image of the heavenly is the resurrection from the dead and incorruption, in order that "as Christ was raised up from the dead by the glory of the Father, so we also should walk in newness of life" [cf. Rom 6:4]. But if anyone were to think that the earthly image is the flesh itself, but the heavenly image some other spiritual body besides the flesh, let him first consider that Christ, the heavenly man, when he appeared, bore the same form of limbs and the same image of flesh as ours, through which also he, who was not man, became man, that "as in Adam all die, so in Christ shall all be made alive" [1 Cor 15:22]. For if he bore flesh for any other reason than that of setting the flesh free and raising it up, why did he bear flesh superfluously? He did not then take the form of a servant uselessly, but to raise it up and save it. For he truly was made man, and died, and not in mere appearance, but that he might truly be shown to be the first begotten from the dead, changing the earthly into the heavenly, and the mortal into the immortal.

(Discourse on the Resurrection 1: based on ANF 6.368)

Commentary: While Origen saw man as yielding in Christ to a subsequent progressive divinization, Methodius thinks much more statically. Like his philosophical master, Aristotle, Methodius feels that there is a place for everything. Thus, everything must be put back together again as in the Genesis story, which he interprets literally. When Christ achieved "incorruption" through his resurrection, the image of God was restored. Christ took human flesh—which is for Methodius on the borderline between corruption and incorruption—and raised it to a condition of incorruption like his own.

2. ATHANASIUS

Introduction

Athanasius, bishop of Alexandria (d. 373), stands as one of the most impressive figures in the whole history of the Christian Church.

His battle against Arianism five times brought him banishment from his See; for more than 17 years he lived in exile. An untiring defender of the faith of the Council of Nicaea (325), he was the teacher *par excellence* of the basic trinitarian and Christological doctrine of the Christian Church. The root of Athanasius' concern for equality of nature between Son and Father lay in his idea of the redemption. Man would not have been redeemed had God not become man and were Christ not God. The physical union of the Word with Christ in the flesh—a flesh in mystic solidarity with all men—makes Christ's humanity a saving humanity and his human acts saving acts. This is the idea of "physical-mystical redemption" found in many of the fathers. For Athanasius, then, the Word achieved the deification of mankind through his assumption of human flesh; he overcame death for all men. Because as Word he was divine, and because of the union between his flesh and man's flesh, his death and victory were in effect the death and victory of man.

A Public Death and a Public Resurrection

"Well then," some people may say, "if the essential thing was that he should surrender his body to death in place of all, why did he not do so as man privately, without going to the length of public crucifixion? Surely it would have been more suitable for him to have laid aside his body with honor than to endure so shameful a death." But it was precisely in order to be able to die that he had taken a body; and to prevent the death would have impeded the resurrection. . . .

The supreme object of his coming was to bring about the resurrection of the body. This was to be the monument to his victory over death, the assurance to all that he had himself conquered corruption and that their own bodies also would eventually be incorrupt; and it was in token of that and as a pledge of the future resurrection that he kept his body incorrupt.

Death had to precede resurrection, for there could be no resurrection without it. A secret and unwitnessed death would have left the resurrection without any proof or evidence to support it. Again, why should he die a secret death, when he proclaimed the fact of his rising openly? Why should he drive out evil spirits and heal the man blind from birth and change water into wine, all publicly, in order to convince men that he was the Word, and not also declare publicly that incorruptibility of his mortal body, so that he might himself be believed to be the Life? And how could his disciples have had boldness in speaking of the resurrection unless they could state it as fact that he had first died? Or how could their hearers be expected to believe their assertion, unless they themselves also had witnessed his death? For if the pharisees at the time refused to believe and forced others to deny also, though the things had happened before their very eyes, how many excuses for unbelief would they have contrived if it had taken place secretly? Or how could the end of death and the victory over it have been declared, had not the Lord thus challenged it before the sight of all, and by the incorruption of his body proved that henceforward it was annulled and void?

(The Incarnation of the Word of God 4.21-23:
based on IWG 50-53)

Commentary: Christ's having a body was the necessary means to his death, says Athanasius, and his death was a necessary means to his resurrection and man's resurrection. Then, too, the resurrection of the body stands as a memorial to Christ's resurrection-victory. For Athanasius, Christ's dying through illness would not work; it would not have been fitting if he who healed others had himself been unhealthy. Yet death was necessary as a step toward Christ's resurrection, and necessary, he says, for apologetic purposes. The death had to be public since the resurrection was openly proclaimed. The public revelation of the restoration was necessary "that he might himself be believed to be the Life." The public resurrection was needed also as a proclamation or a public declaration of "the end of death" and Christ's and man's victory over death.

Conquest of Death

Fitting indeed . . . was the death on the cross for us; and we can see how reasonable it was, and why it is that the salvation of the world could be accomplished in no other way. Even on the cross he did not hide himself from sight; rather, he made all creation witness to the presence of its maker. Then, having once let it be seen that it was truly dead, he did not allow that temple of his body to linger long, but on the third day raised it up, impassible and incorruptible, the pledge and token of his victory.

It was, of course, within his power to have raised his body and displayed it as alive directly after death. But the all-wise savior did not do this, lest some should deny that it was really or completely dead. Besides this, had the interval between his death and resurrection been but two days, the glory of his incorruption might not have appeared. He waited one whole day to show that his body was really dead, and then on the third day showed it incorruptible to all. The interval was no longer, lest people should have forgotten about it and grown doubtful whether it was really the same body. No, while the affair was still ringing in their ears . . . and while those who had put him to death were still on the spot and themselves witnessing to the fact, the Son of God after three days showed his once dead body immortal and incorruptible; and it was evident to all that it was from no natural weakness that the body which the Word indwelled had died, but in order that in [that body] by the savior's power death might be done away with.

A very strong proof of this destruction of death and its conquest by the cross is supplied by a present fact, namely this. All the disciples of Christ despise death; they take the offensive against it and, instead of fearing it, by the sign of the cross and by faith in Christ they trample on it as on something dead. Before . . . even the holiest of men were afraid of death. . . . But now that the savior has raised his body, death is no longer terrible, but all those who believe in Christ tread it underfoot as nothing, and prefer to die rather than to deny their faith in Christ, knowing full well that when they die they do not perish, but live indeed, and become incorruptible through the resurrection. . . . There is proof of this, too; for men who, before they believe in Christ, think death horrible and are afraid of it, once they are converted despise

it so completely that they go eagerly to meet it, and themselves become witnesses of the savior's resurrection from it. Even children hasten thus to die, and not men only, but women train themselves by bodily discipline to meet it. So weak has death become that even women, who used to be taken in by it, mock at it now as a dead thing robbed of all its strength. Death has become like a tyrant who has been completely conquered by the legitimate monarch; bound hand and foot, he is jeered at by the passersby who hit him and abuse him, no longer afraid of his cruelty and rage, because of the king who has conquered him. So has death been conquered and branded for what it is by the savior on the cross. It is bound hand and foot; all who are in Christ trample it as they pass, and as witnesses to him they deride it, scoffing and saying, "O death, where is your victory? O grave, where is your sting?" [1 Cor 15:55].
(Incarnation of the Word 5.26-27: based on IWG 56-58)

> *Commentary:* This passage, with its quaint observations about why the interval was more than one and no longer than three days, reiterates the emphasis of the previous text on the importance of the risen Christ's having good public relations. We notice that Athanasius invokes the experience (very much more immediate to himself and his contemporaries than to us) of martyrdom. And he sees the Christian as completely unafraid of death. In Athanasius' account of the resurrection, the once-exultant wicked old devil and his protégé, that cruel tyrant death, are once and for all put in their places. The patristic imagination was sometimes a bit more vivid than our own.

QUESTIONS FOR DISCUSSION

1. How does Methodius relate Christ's resurrection and man's resurrection? How do his views differ from Origen's?
2. Explain "physical-mystical redemption" as found in Atha-

nasius and other fathers. Is this idea evident in the selections from the *Incarnation of the Word of God?* Explain.
3. Why did Athanasius argue that Christ's death and resurrection had to be public?

CHAPTER 10

CELEBRATION AND

CONFIDENT FAITH

Prefatory Note

The end of the 3rd and the beginning of the 4th centuries saw as occupants of historic Sees Cyril of Jerusalem and John Chrysostom. The first, while unconvincing as a "prophetic" allegorist, effectively communicates his own appreciation of the resurrection. The second is in some ways the most incisive of all the patristic commentators.

1. CYRIL OF JERUSALEM

Introduction

Cyril, who only intermittently acted as bishop of Jerusalem from 348 to his death in 386, was a participant in the First Council of Constantinople (381). His *Catechetical Lectures* are a prime source of information on 4th-century liturgy and sacramental doctrine. Accused of being an Arian early in his career, Cyril is instead theologically anti-Arian. In keeping with the teaching of Nicaea (325), he emphasizes the timeless generation of the Son.

"Free among the Dead"

Be glad, O Jerusalem, and hold festival together, all you who love Jesus, for he is risen; rejoice, all you who before mourned. . . . For he . . . is risen again; and as the lecture on the cross was one of pain, so now let the good tidings of the resurrection gladden all present . . . because of him who after his resurrection said, "Rejoice" [cf. Mt 28:9]. For I know the sorrow of the lovers of Christ during the days past; since . . . not yet having [been] told the good tidings of the resurrection, their mind was kept in suspense to hear what they longed for. Now, therefore, the dead one is risen—he who was "free among the dead" [cf. Ps 88:5] and the deliverer of the dead. He whose head, by reason of his patience, was bound in scorn with the crown of thorns, has now, being risen, put on the diadem of his victory over death.

(Lecture 14.1: based on LFC 165)

Commentary: Cyril begins his lecture on the resurrection, ascension and exaltation of Christ with a kind of hymn of joy. He mistranslates Psalm 88, but his version underlines a truth— the *freedom* of Christ in his resurrection. And the risen Christ wears the diadem of victor over death.

The Winter Is Past

"But unto you have I cried, O Lord, and in the morning shall my prayer come before you" [Ps 88:13]. Do you see how [the prophets] declare the very time both of the passion and of the resurrection? . . .

At what season does the savior arise? Is it the season of summer, or some other? In the [Song of Songs] . . . he [Christ speaking by the prophets] says directly, "The winter is past; the rain is over and gone; the flowers appear on the earth, and the time of pruning is come" [Song 2:11]. Is not the earth now full of flowers, and are they not pruning the vines? You see how he says also that the winter is now past . . . it is now spring; and this season, which is the first month among the Hebrews, is that in which is the feast of the Passover; of the figurative Passover before, but now of the true. This is the season of the creation of the world. For then God said, "Let the earth bring forth grass, the herb yielding seed after his kind" [Gen 1:26]. . . . At that time, God said, "Let us make man in our own image, after our likeness" [Gen 1:26]; and the image he received, but the likeness, by his transgression, he defaced; at that very season, then, in which he lost this, did his restoration also come to pass. At the same season in which created man was cast out of paradise for his disobedience was believing man brought into it again by obeying. Salvation, therefore, was at the very season when the fall of man was, when the flowers appeared and the time of pruning was come.

The place of his burial was a garden, and that which was planted was a vine; for he had said, "And I am the vine" [Jn 15:1]. It was planted then in the earth, that the curse which was on it for Adam's sake might be rooted out. The earth was doomed to thorns and thistles; the true vine sprang out of the earth, that the saying might be fulfilled, "Truth shall spring out of the earth, and righteousness shall look down from heaven" [Ps 85:11]. And what will he say who is buried in the garden? "I have gathered my myrrh with my spice" [Song 5:1] . . . and in the gospels it is said, "The women came to the sepulchre, bringing the spices. . . ." [Lk 24:1] . . . And afterward it is written, "I have eaten my bread with my honey" [Song 5:1], the bitter before his passion, and the sweet after his resurrection. . . . "And they gave him a piece of a broiled fish, and a honeycomb" [cf. Lk 24:42].

(Lecture 14.8, 10-11: based on LFC 168, 170-71)

Commentary: Like some other fathers, Cyril delights in finding "direct prophecies" of detailed features of Christ's resurrection in the Song of Songs. But such so-called "prophecy" does succeed in Cyril as in others in properly conveying truth and mood. The mood here is that of springtime. Cyril appropriately sees the freshness and newness of spring as a context for the *celebration of the resurrection.* Implicit in his parallelism between the springtime of creation and the springtime of the resurrection are some perfectly valid theological truths. Man, who defaced his own likeness to God, has that likeness restored in the resurrection. The resurrection is the re-creation of the likeness of God in man. The disobedience of man is undone and he is restored by Christ's obedience. The resurrection is the time of salvation. And the earth is restored when, in the resurrection, truth rises up from the earth.

2. JOHN CHRYSOSTOM

Introduction

John Chrysostom, who died September 14, 407, had an extraordinary reputation as an orator and teacher of Christian doctrine. Made patriarch of Constantinople against his wishes, John was a notably unsuccessful administrator-bishop, unable to adapt himself to the political realities of the imperial city. A man of extraordinary sincerity and integrity, he died in exile.

His reputation as saint and theologian explains why his extensive literary legacy has been preserved almost totally intact. True to his Antiochene background, Chrysostom was skilled at literal exegesis. His homilies show a distinctively pastoral approach, aimed at illuminating the "spiritual meaning" of scripture passages, and they give us fresh insight into the dynamism of the risen and living Lord. His theology puts unequivocal emphasis on the reality of the two natures in the one Christ.

Filled with His Mighty Power

And while the stones of his tomb were fastened upon the vault, and the seals yet upon them, the dead one arose, the crucified, the nail-pierced one, and having filled his eleven disciples with his mighty power, he sent them to men throughout all the world to be the common healers of their kind, to correct their way of living, to spread through every part of the earth the knowledge of their heavenly doctrines, to bring down the tyranny of devils, to teach those great and unspeakable blessings, to bring to us the glad tidings of the soul's immortality, and the eternal life of the body, and rewards which are beyond conception and shall never have an end.   (Homily 12 on John: based on LFC 1.99)

Commentary: It is the "mighty power" of the risen Christ which fills the disciples as they move out on their missionary tasks. We note that the Gospel which Chrysostom preaches (in view of the resurrection) includes "glad tidings" of immortality, everlasting life and inconceivable "rewards."

Victor over Death and Sin

What especially showed that he was not a mere man was his being able to set up a trophy of victory over death, and thus quickly to abolish his long-enduring tyranny and conclude that difficult war. This is why he said, "Then you shall know." Then! When? When after my resurrection I shall draw the world to me, then you shall know that I did these things as God, and was the true Son of God avenging the insult offered to my Father.   (Homily 23 on John: based on LFC 1.196-97)

Commentary: Here Chrysostom sees the risen Christ as Lord of battles, victorious in the war against death's tyranny and triumphant avenger over sin.

A Daily Resurrection

"Always bearing about in our body the Lord Jesus, that the life also of Jesus might be manifested in our body" [2 Cor 4:10]. And what is the dying of the Lord Jesus, which they bear about? Their daily death, in which the resurrection was also shown. "For if any do not believe," he says, "that Jesus died and rose again, beholding us every day die and rise again, let them believe henceforward in the resurrection."
                    (Homily 9 on 2 Corinthians: based on LFC 1.117)

Commentary: This is a good example of Chrysostom's careful pastoral exploration of a scripture text. John argues that the daily death of Christ's disciples shows a person who does not yet believe in Christ that Christ died and rose again. Christ's resurrection is "proved" by Christian man's everyday, this-worldly resurrection.

"Not for One Only But for All"

"That he who raised the Lord Jesus, shall raise us also with Jesus and bring us with you into his presence. For it is all for your sake, so that the abundant grace might through the thanksgiving of many redound to the glory of God" (2 Cor 4:14-15). Again, he fills them with noble thoughts, but they may not hold themselves indebted to men—I mean to the false apostles. For the whole is of God, who wills to bestow [grace] upon many, so that [it] may appear the greater. For your sakes, therefore, was the resurrection and all the other things. For he did not do these things for the sake of one only, but for all.   (Homily 9 on 2 Corinthians: based on LFC 1.117)

> *Commentary:* Man's debt is not to human beings but to the Father "who raised the Lord Jesus." The grace of resurrection is entirely from God, and in no sense from men. The resurrection of Christ, moreover, is a gift of the Father given not only for Christ's sake but for *all*.

By Faith Alone

But what is this faith? "By faith," he says, "that I may know him" [Phil 3:10]; so, then, the knowledge is by faith, and without faith it is impossible to know him. But how? Through it we must know the power of his resurrection. For what reasoning can demonstrate to us the resurrection? None, but faith only. For if the resurrection of Christ, who existed according to the flesh, is known by faith, how can the generation of the Word of God be comprehended by reasoning? For the resurrection is less than the generation. And how? Of that there have been many examples, but of this not one: for many dead have arisen before Christ, though after their resurrection they die, but no one was ever born of a virgin. If, then, we must comprehend by faith that which is inferior to the generation according to the flesh, how can that which is far greater, immeasurably and incomparably greater, be comprehended by reason? . . . We must believe that he was able, but how he was able we cannot prove. For from faith is the fellowship of his sufferings. But how? Had we not believed, neither should we have suffered; had we not believed that "if we suffer with him, we shall also reign with him" [cf. 2 Tim 2:12], we should not have endured the sufferings. Wherefore both the generation and resurrection are comprehended by faith. Do you not see that faith must not be absolutely, but through good works, for that man especially believes that Christ has risen, who in like sort gives himself up to dangers, who has fellowship with him in his sufferings. For he has fellowship with him who rose again, with him who lives; wherefore he says, "that I may be found in him, not having a righteousness of my own, based on law, but that which is through faith in Christ, the righteousness from God which depends on faith; that I may know him and the power of his resurrection, and may share his sufferings, being made conformable to his death, that if possible I may attain the resurrection of the dead" [Phil 3:9-11]. He says, being made conformable unto his death, i.e., having fellowship; whereas he suffered from men, thus I, too; wherefore he says, "being made conformable," and again in another place, "and in my flesh I complete what is lacking in Christ's afflictions" [Col 1:24], i.e., in persecutions. For these persecutions and sufferings work that image of his death, for he sought not his own, but the good of many.

Therefore, persecutions and afflictions and straits ought not to disturb you, but even make you glad, because through them we are "conformed to his death." As if he had said, we are molded to his likeness; as he says in another place, where he writes "bearing about in the body the dying of the Lord Jesus" [2 Cor 4:10]. And this, too, comes from great faith. For we not only believe that he arose, but that after his resurrection also he has great power: wherefore we travel the

same road which he traveled, i.e., we become brethren to him in this respect. How great is the dignity of suffering!
(Homily 11 on Philippians [3:7-10]: based on LFC 131-32)

Commentary: Here Chrysostom unequivocally states a proposition most traditional apologists, along with certain writers of historic Church documents, would be unable to accept: The resurrection of Christ is known to us only by faith; we cannot know it through "rational proof" or demonstration. The difference between these writers and Chrysostom is that he has scripture solidly on his side. Furthermore, Chrysostom takes faith in the resurrection not as a conclusion but as an obvious starting point in his argument that the generation of the Word must also be known by faith.

Chrysostom ties his whole complex argument in with the Christian's conviction that endurance of suffering is only acceptable in terms of sharing in Christ's suffering—and that what this sharing ultimately means is sharing with Christ in resurrection: "We shall also reign with him." There is a difference, however, between sharing in Christ's suffering and sharing in his resurrection. Community with Christ in suffering is a community with him who once suffered but *now no longer suffers.* But community with him who rose again is community with the Christ who *"now lives."* The reason for "being made conformable to Christ's death" is that the Christian "may know him and the power of his resurrection." Man's suffering, by identifying him with the past suffering of the Lord Jesus, brings man *by faith* into contact with the *risen* Christ and with the *power* of the risen Christ.

In summary, then: For Chrysostom, man moves along a road whose term is union with the living Christ—not the suffering, but the risen Christ. The great dignity of Christian suffering lies in this: that through his endurance of suffering with Christ, the Christian transcends suffering; the Christ he here comes in contact with is the risen, living Lord in all his power.

Types of the Resurrection

Christ was to rise again; see now how many sure signs there were of this: Enoch, Elijah, Jonah, the fiery furnace, the baptism that happened in Noah's day, the seeds, the plants, our own generation, that of all animals. For since in this everything was at stake, it more than any other had abundance of types.

(Homily 4 on Colossians: based on LFC 244-45)

Commentary: Though Chrysostom preferred not to do excessive allegorizing and though he seems not to have pressed the Old Testament for "prophetic" meanings it did not contain (here he differs from the highly ambitious allegorists of Alexandria), he is perceptive in searching out highlights of anticipation— signs he finds in nature, as well as in scripture, which point in a rich variety of ways to the resurrection, and which relate to it as symbols and types.

The Power of the Living Christ

For in reality it is the greatest proof of the resurrection that the slain Christ should show forth so great power after death as to persuade living men to despise both country and home and friends . . . and life itself for the sake of confessing him, and to choose, in place of present pleasures, stripes and dangers and death. For these are not the achievements of any dead man, nor of one remaining in the tomb, but of one risen and living, since how could you account, when he was alive, for all the apostles who accompanied him becoming weaker through fear to betray their teacher and to flee and depart; but when he died, for not only Peter and Paul, but even Ignatius, who had not even seen him or enjoyed his companionship, showing such earnestness as to lay down life itself for his sake?

(Homily on St. Ignatius: based on NPNF 9.139)

Commentary: Here Chrysostom argues characteristically that Christ's resurrection is proved by nothing so much as by Christian heroism. The willingness of men to lay down their lives for his sake cannot be attributed to some dead man. This achievement in men can only testify to a Christ who is risen and living. It was precisely after his death that the apostles and other, later disciples really became courageous. This is inexplicable if Christ merely remained dead, for his death could (and did) only confirm them in their fear.

QUESTIONS FOR DISCUSSION

1. How does Cyril of Jerusalem use Old Testament materials to interpret Christ's resurrection and its relation to man? Give a few illustrations and show how they are effective.
2. In what ways is Chrysostom "pastoral" in his exploration of scripture texts on Christ's resurrection?
3. On what basis does Chrysostom express the Christian conviction of Christ's resurrection? How does Chrysostom defend the dignity of Christian suffering? Explain.
4. How does Chrysostom "prove" the resurrection of Christ?

CHAPTER 11
IMMORTAL AND
EVERLASTING LIFE

Prefatory Note

In this chapter are joined what some would consider strange bed-fellows: Theodore, some of whose writings were considered heretical after his death in the wake of Cyril's Nestorian purge, and Cyril himself, an accomplished politician and pillar of orthodoxy—yet a man whose stress on Christological unity won him the dubious but not wholly undeserved honor (also *post-mortem*) of being declared the great doctor of the monophysites.

1. THEODORE OF MOPSUESTIA

Introduction

At his death in 428, Theodore was widely respected and venerated for his learning and orthodoxy. His ideas were in a sense condemned 125 years later due to their association with the Nestorian heresy. Yet it was only by distorting his words and their context that his posthumous critics could really build much of a case against Theodore. Theodore does, of course, emphasize the human activity of what he called "the assumed man"— Christ (a more refined theology would say) in his human nature. Theodore, from his very deep appreciation of the meaning of Christ's *human manhood,* sees Christ not only as the bringer of salvation and of the "second age" of immortality; Christ is also in his human nature the *object* of God's salvation. He is the "pathfinder" or "pioneer" precisely in being the first to move across the frontier between the present life and the life of the age to come. "The man's" union with God the Word won the redemption he generously bestows on others. Theodore sees Christ progressing or developing toward the goal of the age to come, the second age. In this progressive movement, his death and resurrection together constitute the decisive events.

Transformation of Christ's Humanity

Our Lord Jesus Christ, assumed from us and for us, died according to the human law and has become, by virtue of the resurrection, immortal, incorruptible and absolutely immutable.

(Catechetical Homily 12.6: Norris 196)

Commentary: Christ's manhood, taken from men for men's sake, and subjected to death in line with his human condition, is totally transformed and given attributes of divine permanence in his resurrection.

Two Ages of Human Existence

This was indeed God's pleasure—to divide the whole creation into two stages: the present one in which he made everything mutable, and the one which will be, when by renewing everything he will transfer it to immutability. The foundation of these things he shows us in the dispensation of the Lord Christ, whom as taking his existence from among us he raised from the dead and made immutable in body and soul. Through this he demonstrated that this would happen to the entire creation.

(Commentary on Genesis: based on Greer 72-73)

Commentary: Here Theodore points to two ages of human existence: (1) the present age is changeable (because of man's freedom); (2) the immutable age is in the future. The starting point of this future age is Christ who by his resurrection is now immortal and unchangeable in glory. Theodore concludes here on a characteristic note of optimism: the resurrection of Christ is a pledge of the transformation of the whole creation.

Christ as the Pledge of Man's Resurrection

The things the ancients held as figures and shadows now become reality when our Lord Jesus Christ—who was assumed from us and for us died according to the human law, and through his resurrection became immortal, incorruptible and forever immutable, and as such ascended into heaven—by his union with our nature became to us an earnest of our own participation in the event. . . . Since we have a firm belief that things that have already happened will happen to us, so we believe [the things that happened at the resurrection of our Lord] will happen to us.

> (Catechetical Homily on the Nicene Creed:
> based on Greer 74)

Commentary: The risen Christ is looked upon as a pledge or guarantee that what happened to him (his resurrection) also "will happen to us." The risen Lord prefigures personally the future age of resurrection that will come to those hoping and believing in Christ.

2. CYRIL OF ALEXANDRIA

Introduction

Cyril, bishop of Alexandria from 412 to 444, was perhaps more a political than a theological victor over Nestorius in the Christological battle which culminated in Nestorius' condemnation at Ephesus. Cyril's own formulations about Christ's nature and person were ambiguous, and so open to misunderstanding that later on the monophysites would refer to Cyril as their great doctor. But from the problems that arose from Cyril's use of "one nature" in speaking of Christ, it becomes clear that he placed the unity of Christ in Christ's person and did not deny what the Council of Chalcedon would call a duality of natures. Nestorius' own insights live on in the Church today in the current de-emphasis of the prerogatives of Mary and in the current emphasis on the humanity of Christ. (On the Cyril-Nestorius controversies, see Carmody-Clarke, *Word and Redeemer* [GTF 2, Glen Rock, N.J., 1966], esp. pp. 81-99.) In some of his commentaries, Cyril is blissfully detached from Greek metaphysical concerns and speaks of Christ almost wholly in biblical categories.

Christ as Forerunner

Christ was numbered among the dead, who for our sake became dead, according to the flesh, but whom we conceive to be, and who is, in fact, life, of himself and through his Father. And that he might fulfill all righteousness, that is, all that was appropriate to the form of man, he of his own will subjected the temple of his body not merely to death, but also to what follows after death, that is, burial and being laid in the tomb. The writer of the Gospel says that this sepulchre in the garden was a new one, this fact signifying to us . . . that Christ's death is the harbinger and pioneer of our entry into paradise. For he "entered as a forerunner for us" [Heb 6:20]. And by the newness of the sepulchre is meant the untrodden and strange pathway whereby we return from death unto life, and the renewing of our souls, that Christ has invented for us, whereby we baffle corruption. For henceforth, by the death of Christ, death for us has been transformed, in a manner, into sleep, with like power and functions. For we are "alive unto God" [Rom 6:11] and shall live forevermore, according to the scriptures. Therefore, also, the blessed Paul in a variety of places describes as "asleep" those who have died in Christ. For in ancient times the dread presence of death held human nature in awe. . . . But when the second Adam appeared among us, the divine man from heaven, and, contending for the salvation of the world, purchased by his death the life of all men, and, destroying the power of corruption, rose again to life, we were transformed into his image. And we undergo, as it were, a different kind of death that does not dissolve us in eternal corruption, but casts upon us a slumber which is full of fair hope, after the likeness of him who has made this new path for us, that is, Christ. And if anyone choose to give an additional meaning to the saying that the sepulchre was a new one, and that no man had been laid therein, be it so. He says, then, we may suppose, that the sepulchre was new, and that no one had been ever laid therein, that no one might be thought to have arisen from the sleep of death, save Jesus only.

(Commentary 12 on John: based on LFC 2.647–48)

Commentary: Cyril here uses an image, prominent in other fathers, of Christ as the forerunner or "pioneer," almost as though he were preaching the Gospel to American settlers of the 19th century. Christ, in his death, burial and resurrection, leads man into paradise. It is a strange uncharted trail, the trail from death to life. In Christ our death becomes like a sleep. In the new country men wake to "live forevermore," transformed into the image of the second man, the "divine man from heaven," who destroys the power of corruption in his resurrection to life. Working in the allegorical tradition of Alexandria with his idea of man as transformed into the image of God through Christ, he sees the newness of the sepulchre as a symbol of the uniqueness of Jesus as savior.

Woman: "Crowned with a Double Honor"

"But go to my brethren, and say to them, 'I ascend to my Father and your Father, and my God and your God' " [Jn 20: 17]. . . . Christ does not permit Mary to touch him, although in her love for God she greatly yearned for this blessing; but he still rewards her for her watchful care and doubly rewards her for her passionate faith and love for him, showing that those who are diligent in his service meet with a recompense. And even still more glorious, she achieved the deliverance of woman from the frailties of old; for first in her

—I mean in Mary [Magdalene]—all womankind, so to speak, is crowned with a double honor. For though she at first grieved this way, and made Christ an occasion for weeping, she turned her mourning into joy when she was told to stop weeping—by him who by his own ancient decree had made woman an easy mark for the attacks of sorrow. For God had said to the woman: "In sorrow you shall bring forth children" [Gen 3:16]. But just as he once made her subject to sorrow in paradise, when she listened to the voice of the serpent and ministered to the devil's tricks, so now, again in a garden, he asks her to stop weeping. Releasing her from that curse which [sentenced] her to sorrow, he calls her to be the first messenger of tidings of great joy, and to proclaim to the disciples his journey heavenward; so that just as the first woman, the mother of all mankind, was condemned for listening to the devil's voice—and through her the whole race of women—so also this woman, in her listening to our savior's words and her proclamation of tidings pregnant with eternal life, might deliver the entire race of women from the charge of old.

(Commentary 12 on John: based on LFC 2.661–62)

Commentary: Many expositors of "Christian" tradition were at one with Cyril in seeing woman as something of a menace to male humanity. Cyril saw her not only as the daughter of Eve, but also as a "constantly chattering creature," with a special talent for "deceitfulness" (cf. PG 68.205). But in contrast to most other early writers, he sees her also as a redeeming influence, with Mary Magdalene here as the bearer and symbol of woman's new honor.

QUESTIONS FOR DISCUSSION

1. What emphasis do we find in Theodore of Mopsuestia's theology? How does this reflect his view on the meaning of Christ's resurrection? Explain.

2. What two ages of human existence does Theodore point out? How are these related to Christ's resurrection?

3. What was Cyril of Alexandria trying to emphasize by using "one nature" in speaking of Christ?

4. What meaning does Cyril find in the newness of the sepulchre in which Christ was laid? What was he trying to express by the image of Christ as forerunner or "pioneer"?

5. What does Cyril have to say about Mary Magdalene?

CHAPTER 12

UNION IN NEW
LIFE AND FREEDOM

Prefatory Note

Our survey of the fathers' teaching on the resurrection would be necessarily incomplete without a look at Ambrose and Augustine, two great Latin fathers of the late 4th and early 5th centuries. Ambrose was a decisive influence on the younger Augustine; both were men of great sensitivity—bishops for whom, amid administrative problems, pastoral concern was paramount.

1. AMBROSE

Introduction

St. Ambrose, who died in 397, was in 373 (shortly after his baptism) made bishop of Milan, an office which, under pressure from both Christians and Arians, he accepted only reluctantly. In Ambrose's Christology the divine and human natures of Christ were held neatly in balance, in line with the "safe" Western tradition. His treatises *On the Sacraments* (some have challenged Ambrose's authorship of this work, attributing it, for example, to Maximus of Turin) and *On the Mysteries* show us a theme often found in the fathers but rarely expressed with such eloquence: In baptism the Christian is identified in newness of life with the risen Jesus.

Baptism as Burial and Resurrection

Yesterday we discussed the [baptismal] font, whose appearance is somewhat like that of a tomb in shape; into which, believing in the Father and the Son and the Holy Spirit, we are received, and plunged, and we emerge, that is, we are raised up. Moreover, you receive myrrh, that is, ointment, upon the head. Why upon the head? Because "the senses of a wise man are in his head," says Solomon. For wisdom is lifeless without grace; but when wisdom has received grace, then its work begins to be perfect. This is called regeneration.

(On the Sacraments 3.1: based on Srawley 70)

> *Commentary:* The baptized and anointed Christian is raised up and his wisdom made living and perfect. The total effect is regeneration. The tomb-shaped font and the rite of immersion clearly reflect the symbolism of burial and resurrection with Christ.

Christ's Birth as Son

What is regeneration? You read in the Acts of the Apostles that the verse which is found in the second psalm, "You are my Son; this day have I begotten you," appears to refer to the resurrection. For the holy apostle Peter in the Acts of the Apostles interpreted it thus: that at the time that the Son rose from the dead, the Father's voice rang out, "You are my Son; this day have I begotten you" [cf. Acts 13:33]. Therefore, he is also called "the firstborn from the dead" [Col 1:18]. Therefore, what is resurrection, but when we rise from death to life? So, therefore, in baptism also, since there is a likeness of death, without doubt when you dip and rise again, there is a likeness of the resurrection. Rightly, therefore, according to the interpretation of the apostle Peter, as that resurrection was a regeneration, so also is this resurrection a regeneration.

(On the Sacraments 3.2-3: based on Srawley 70-71)

Commentary: Ambrose here reiterates a theme found in many fathers, as well as in the New Testament: Christ's birth as the Son comes at the time of his resurrection. This rebirth, this regeneration, makes Christ the *first* to be born from the dead. He stresses the note of rebirth from *death*, of regeneration as resurrection from death. The Christian in baptism is risen and regenerated on the model of Christ's resurrection and regeneration.

Daily Resurrection

"Give us this day our daily bread." If you receive daily, "this day" is "daily" to you. If Christ is for you "this day," he rises again for you "daily." How? "You are my Son; this day have I begotten you" [Ps 2:7]. Therefore "this day" is when Christ rises again. "Yesterday and today he himself is" [Heb 13:8], says the apostle Paul. But in another place he says, "The night is far spent; the day is at hand" [Rom 13:12]. Last night is far spent; the present day is at hand.

(On the Sacraments 5.26: based on Srawley 105-06)

Commentary: Ambrose here argues directly for daily reception of the eucharist. Christ rises again for the person who receives him "this day."

2. AUGUSTINE

Introduction

Augustine, an African and the bishop of Hippo, the greatest of the Latin fathers and probably the most influential teacher for good and for ill in the entire history of Christian theology, died in the year 430, leaving a vast body of literature behind him. No writer of the patristic age has left us so large a volume of material on the meaning of the resurrection, and much the same could be said of many another patristic theme.

From Death to Life

The resurrection of our Lord Jesus Christ betokens a new life for those who believe in Jesus, and that is the mystery of his passion and his resurrection, a fact that ought to loom ever larger both in your awareness and in your conduct. Not without reason did he drink of that chalice which he in no way deserved—he who is the font of life from which we drink in order to have life.

Let us inquire into the origin of death. . . . Had there not been sin there would not be death. For the first man . . . committed the act which brought about his death, and thus was made to feel the truth of the warning spoken by the lawgiver. There we have the origin of death following on the first, that is to say, eternal death following in the wake of temporal death. Every man born is bound by this tradition of death, by this law of perdition, except that man who became man that mankind might not perish. For he was born not subject to the law of death, as is said in the psalm, "A free man among the dead" [Ps 88:5].

For this reason he was crucified, that on the cross he might show us the new life which is ours. . . . For so we are instructed by the apostle's teaching, where he says, "He was delivered up for our sins, and rose again for our justification" [Rom 4:25]. As a sign thereof, circumcision was given to our forefathers—that is, on the eighth day every male child had to be circumcised [cf. Gen 17:12]. Circumcision was performed with knives of flint [cf. Jos 5:2], "for the rock was Christ" [1 Cor 10:4]. In that circumcision was prefigured the destruction of our carnal life through the resurrection of Christ on the eighth day. For the seventh day of the week terminated with the Sabbath. On the Sabbath, the seventh day of the week, our Lord lay in the tomb. He arose on the eighth day. And since his resurrection restores us to new life, he circumcises us, in a sense, by rising from the dead on the eighth day. In this very hope we now live.

(Sermon 20: based on Weller 152-53)

Commentary: New life for those who believe in Jesus is pledged by the resurrection of Christ. Death is the progeny of sin; it followed from disobedience to the Law. The Law therefore is, as death-bringing, "this law of perdition" from which Christ, as free man among the dead, was exempt. Augustine also finds a symbol and a symbolic date in the Israelite custom of circumcision on the eighth day. Even the flint used in circumcision symbolizes Christ as the rock. Augustine argues that since circumcision involves destruction of what is fleshly, it prefigures Christ's resurrection seen as Christian man's circumcision—meaning that in Christ's resurrection man puts off his old "carnal" life and is brought or restored to new life.

Christ's Resurrection as Redemption

But once sin had created a wide rift between the human race and God, it was necessary that a mediator . . . should reconcile us with God . . . so that man in his stubbornness might receive an example of obedience from the God-man; and so that the fountain of grace might be opened by the only-begotten taking the form of a servant, a form which had no antecedent merits; and so that the resurrection also of the body, promised to the redeemed, might be presaged in the resurrection of the redeemer; and so that the devil might be conquered by that same nature which he rejoiced to have deceived, without man, however, taking glory in himself, lest pride spring up anew.

(Enchiridion 108: based on ACW 3.102)

Commentary: Augustine sees Christ's mediation as *exemplary* in his obedience, as *efficient* in his servanthood, as *anticipatory* in his resurrection. Here Christ's resurrection functions as an announcement or proclamation of the resurrection of the body. Important to Augustine is the idea that man is redeemed through Christ's resurrection without any merit on man's part, yet redeemed in Christ's human nature.

God's Power in the Resurrection

But you, whoever you are, who prefer to glory in power rather than in humiliation, be consoled and be filled with jubilation. For he who was crucified under Pontius Pilate and was buried arose from the dead on the third day. Perhaps you also doubt this; perhaps you are wavering. When you were told to believe that he was born, to believe that he suffered, was crucified, died and was buried, you believed this readily enough, since he was man. But now that it is said he arose from the dead on the third day, are you doubtful? Of the many arguments that could be brought forth, let us concentrate on this one: Remember that he is God, reflect that he is almighty, and have no doubt about it. For if before you existed he could make you out of nothing, then why could he not raise from the dead the humanity already brought into being by him? Believe this, my brethren, for when it is a question of faith, it is not necessary to go on at length.

It is faith in the resurrection that alone sets apart and distinguishes Christians from all other men. For even the pagans now believe that he died and was buried, and the Jews witnessed [these things]. But that he arose from the dead on the third day, neither the pagan nor the Jew admits. Therefore, belief in the resurrection of the dead is what distinguished the life of our faith from the deadly state of unbelievers. As the apostle Paul wrote to Timothy, "Be mindful that the Lord Jesus Christ is risen again from the dead" [2 Tim 2:8]. Therefore, brethren, let us believe and let us hope that what happened to Christ will also happen to us. For God who makes a promise does not deceive.

(Sermon 30: based on Weller 220-21)

Commentary: Augustine says that there is something for those who appreciate power (in contradistinction to those Augustine seems to prefer—those who glory in humiliation): Christ's resurrection testifies to divine power in him.

Augustine, like Chrysostom, stresses the need for *belief* in the resurrection. Augustine's only *argument* is a suasive one—

that while the events of Christ's life are more readily believed (since Christ was a man), creation out of nothing is more incredible than the raising of a pre-existent personality.

But Augustine is really not interested in arguing the resurrection. It is a matter of faith. This faith is the distinctive mark of Christians. The resurrection is really all that is left to believe, if death and burial are taken as the Gospel presents them—as events obvious to everyone. Living in faith in the resurrection, Augustine again insists, means living in the confident conviction of a personal resurrection like Christ's.

From Double Death to Double Life

We certainly . . . are dead both in soul and body: in soul because of sin; in body because of the punishment of sin, and through this also in body because of sin. And for both these parts of ourselves . . . there was need both of a medicine and of resurrection, so that what had been changed for the worse might be renewed for the better. Now the death of the soul is ungodliness, and the death of the body is corruptibility—through which there also comes a departure of the soul from the body. . . . The soul is raised up again by repentance, and the renewing of life is begun in the still mortal body by faith, by which men believe in him who justified the ungodly. . . .

Therefore, in view of this double death of ours, our savior gave his own single death. And to cause our double-resurrection he appointed beforehand and set forth in mystery and type his own resurrection.

(On the Trinity 4.3: based on NPNF 3.72)

Commentary: Man needs healing and resurrection so that he may be renewed in both soul and body. Renewal of man's soul means his being raised up from ungodliness to justification; renewal of man's body means his being raised from corruptibility to incorrupt life. It is important to see that Augustine views the resurrection as both (a) a type, exemplar or pattern of man's resurrection, and (b) a mystery into which man in his risen life is and will be plunged.

"There Shall Be No Deformity"

Overgrown and emaciated persons need not fear that they shall be in heaven of such a figure as they would not be even in this world if they could help it. For all bodily beauty consists in the proportion of the parts, together with a certain agreeableness of color. Where there is no proportion, the eye is offended, either because there is something wanting, or too small, or too large. And thus there shall be no deformity resulting from want of proportion in that state in which all that is wrong is corrected, and all that is defective supplied from resources the creator knows of, and all that is excessive removed without destroying the integrity of the substance. And as for the pleasant color, how conspicuous shall it be where "the just shine forth as the sun in the kingdom of their Father" [Mt 13:43]. This brightness we must rather believe to have been concealed from the eyes of the disciples when Christ rose, than to have been wanting. For weak human eyesight could not bear it, and it was necessary that they should so look upon him as to be able to recognize him.

(City of God 22.19: based on NPNF 2.497-98)

Commentary: Augustine shows himself in the *City of God* to be full of ideas about just how men might *look* after their resurrection. He has opinions on height (probably gigantic), weight (fat people will be trimmed down and thin ones fleshed out), age (perhaps 30) and various other particulars. Augustine is here very much in the Western, Tertullianist, literal school of thinking. In the passage above, Augustine considers problems of size and color, using a subtle aesthetic of proportion as his norm. Measuring the brightness of the resurrection body leads him naturally into vexing questions about just how radiant the risen Christ might have seemed. Augustine apparently thinks Christ was not as "turned on" as he might have been.

QUESTIONS FOR DISCUSSION

1. How does Ambrose present Christian baptism? How does he connect Christ's birth as Son and baptism?
2. What connection does Ambrose make between Christ's resurrection and Christian reception of the eucharist?
3. How does Augustine relate death and sin? Does he think that man is redeemed through Christ's resurrection without any merit on man's part? Explain.
4. According to Augustine, what is it that sets apart and distinguishes Christians from all other men?
5. What does Augustine mean when he speaks of man's "double death"? How is man to be saved from this?

CONCLUSION

REVELATION

WITHIN A MYSTERY

Among the later fathers not covered in the present study, Maximus the Confessor (d. 662) was an expert synthesist. Maximus was especially concerned with Christ's resurrection as a revelation to man of the total mystery of Christianity. This total mystery includes for Maximus man's risen life, a life which brings with it divinization or deification, both in the present existence and in the afterlife.

To Maximus, then, it is of utmost importance for understanding the ultimate direction of creation that men go beyond Christ's death and burial: "He who penetrates beyond the cross and the tomb and finds himself initiated into the mystery of the resurrection, learns the end for which God has created everything" (PG 91.1392).

The revelation of the mystery of the resurrection can, as we have seen, be distinguished into two different aspects: the revelation of the meaning of Christ's own person, and the revelation of creation's meaning, especially man's.

Judgment and Vengeance

Beginning with the second aspect, let us review some of the highlights of the fathers' teaching. The *Didache,* which presumes rather than proclaims the resurrection of Christ, is marked by the expectation of a rather immediate second coming of Christ. He is not only Lord and Son of man; he is also "judge"; we have heavy emphasis here, in keeping with the moralistic nature of the *Didache,* on moral preparation: only some will rise—those who have met the "fiery test" by a kind of stoic "standing firm in their faith." As in apocalyptic and moralizing passages of the New Testament, there is a feeling of impending persecution. The challenge to firm moral readiness suggests that believers may have to face martyrdom. Polycarp carried forward the moral emphasis of the *Didache* here on two points: Man's acts are the test of whether *or not* man rises; God through Jesus Christ is judge —and a judge who will *avenge* Christ's blood on the disobedient. The "Letter of Barnabas" also has Christ's resurrection as preparing him for judgeship. Justin has fiery punishment awaiting enemies of the Gospel. Irenaeus similarly envisions eternal fire for "the godless and wicked and lawless and blasphemers." For both, the resurrection of Christ is an intermediate step toward both resurrection and life (for the just) and triumphant punishment (for evildoers). Hippolytus sees the resurrection as establishing Christ's power as judge and arbiter. Tertullian's Christ is slightly sadistic and more than slightly vengeful: Christ avoids the general public after the resurrection so that the faithful, "destined to a great reward," will retain their faith amid difficulty, and "to prevent the wicked from being delivered from their error." Cyprian sees Christ's resurrection as a pattern of victory only for Christians; he denies salvation to those outside the Church.

Christ's Victory as Man's Victory

Apart from such instances, however, the fathers are quite positive in their view of the effects of Christ's resurrection on men. There is, considering the times, a quite surprising stress on its benefits. Origen, for example, has Christ as divine judge, but a judge whose function seems to be to range the human and angelic world in search of converts—i.e., to get wrongdoers gradually set straight (here or hereafter) so that they will not have to endure eternal punishment.

For Clement of Rome, God "the Master" is ever busy calling men's attention to the final resurrection, of which Christ's resurrection is the first harvest. Ignatius and the author of the "Martyrdom of Polycarp" see death as a preparation for resurrection to eternal life. In Melito the risen Christ invites all the "families of men" to receive in him remission of sins. He is their passover, their ransom, their light, their savior, who will lead them "up to the heights of the heavens." Methodius cites Paul's text (1 Cor 15:22), "As in Adam all die, so in Christ shall all be made alive," and insists that the reason Christ bore flesh was so that he could set human flesh free and raise it up, giving it incorruption. To Athanasius, it is not right that men who had once shared God's own image should be destroyed. The Word came as the perfect image of the Father to publicly vanquish death, and in his incorruption and immortality to bring men to incorruption through the resurrection. Cyril of Jerusalem sees Christ as "free among the dead," ransoming and redeeming men from the power of death. Chrysostom sees men, healed and "corrected" by the Gospel, as given immortality, life and inconceivable "rewards" through Christ's mighty power. After his resurrection, Christ, victor in the war with death, draws the world to himself. Christ rose for the sake of all. Theodore of Mopsuestia views man as of himself encompassed with weakness and mortality; the Lord Jesus Christ, who became through his resurrection immortal, incorruptible and immutable, confers on man a second life, a new, immortal and sinless life. Cyril of Alexandria sees Christ, rising from a new sepulchre, as the forerunner of a new life for man. The divine man from heaven purchases men's life by his death and transforms men into his image by his resurrection. For Ambrose, Christ is first of the dead to be born as Son; in baptism Christians follow him in regeneration to new life. The "this day I have begotten you" of scripture applies to man on the day of his baptism and on any day he receives the eucharist, as it applied to Christ on the day of his resurrection. For Augustine,

the resurrection is the mystery of Christ's and man's passover from death to life. In Christ's resurrection, man, who
has no merit of his own, is directly justified through restoration to new life; he is freed from death and bondage to sin,
delivered from ungodliness to incorrupt life.

Christ's Resurrection and Man's Resurrection

Two conclusions stand out from what we have seen: (1)
None of the fathers see the resurrection of Christ as an event
that happened to and for Christ alone. *All men are affected
by it.* (2) Some see it, of course, as chiefly or partly paving
the way for man's condemnation in his wickedness. But the
stronger testimony is to the resurrection as *Christ's pioneering
movement in the drama of man's progress from death to life.*
Some fathers apply this exclusively to members of the
Church. Some—like Origen, Melito, Athanasius and Chrysostom—envision, or tend to make more allowance for, a
wider resurrection community.

To Know Christ Risen

How are men to know the risen Lord? If we incorporate the
testimony of later fathers like Chrysostom and Augustine with
the early testimony of Ignatius (and see him together with
fathers like Athanasius and Ambrose), we come to a conclusion that runs somewhat like this: To know Christ as
risen Lord, we must know him in person, through faith. Our
knowledge is a knowledge in terms of confession of him as
personal savior. There is no objective, independent "rational"
knowledge of the resurrection. The resurrection is known as
factual in the context of this transubjective personal knowledge. It is unassailably certain knowledge, but only to him
who at the same time believes. These fathers, faithful to the
spirit of the first Christian community, know assuredly that
God the Father raised Jesus from the dead and made him
both Lord and Christ. They know this only—yet know it

certainly—through their commitment to and contact with the risen Lord who lives and himself speaks to them. "You never saw him," Polycarp writes to the Philippians, "and yet you believe in him with sublime and inexpressible joy."

The secret, then, is the personal presence of him who rose and is now alive in his mighty power. "There is in me a living water, which within me says, 'Come to the Father,'" writes Ignatius. There is no separation between the personal Christ and his resurrection: "Him I love who rose again because of us."

The Presence of the Risen Christ

Origen sees the resurrection of Christ in terms of his present experience of the Lord who "ranges the world," gathering and attracting a people "by his divinity." Christians know the resurrection in confessing the Christ who is present to them. This they show in their prayers of praise, as when Ambrose addresses the Father "through his only-begotten Son, our Lord God, king and savior, through whom and with whom to him is praise, honor, glory, majesty, power . . . both now and forever. . . ." Through the sacraments, through the Word, through life lived in Christ, Christians are continually reinitiated into the mystery.

It is therefore futile to argue. No proofs will supply assurance to those who do not see. Ignatius on his way to martyrdom wrote something that should have cut off from the beginning any attempts to "prove" to non-Christians the resurrection or anything else about Christ from the Old Testament scriptures. These "archives" are relatively unimportant; the living person alone is really significant: "To me the official record is Jesus Christ."

Apologetic Efforts

Many other fathers were at pains to supply "helps" in the form of natural and Old Testament analogies, metaphors, testimonies, signs, and so on. We saw Clement of Rome using Old Testament texts, some of them obscure, to "call attention" (much as natural "examples" are supposed to) to the "sublime promise" of the resurrection. Clement, writing to Christians, does not try to *prove* man's resurrection from these texts or examples; Christ's resurrection seems to supply the basis for assurance. "Barnabas" sees Christ's passion and resurrection as fulfilling the promise made to Abraham and the patriarchs. This is quite legitimate usage in a Christian instruction; the Christ-events are for Christians the fulfillment of those "promises." But Justin is on quite other and shakier ground in trying to use the psalms as arguments to convince pagans—his imperial audience must have wondered—and in speaking of Psalm 110 as a "prediction" of Christ's resurrection to power and his mighty missionary Word. Justin was no more compassionate with the Jews, and was anything but ecumenical in his attempt to prove that the Jonah story plus the use of it in Matthew as a resurrection metaphor clearly equaled a message to the Jews to repent, to quit cursing Christians and to join them.

Origen lifts tradition (e.g., the blessings of the firstborn) and institutions (the temple) and people (Abraham) from the Old Testament and uses them as he pleases to fashion contrasts or anticipations or parallels for the edification of his Christian hearers. He appropriates whole books (e.g., the Song of Songs) to remake them over into allegories of Christian teaching. He does this with such exuberance that he has often been criticized for his wholesale allegorism. Yet he does not take himself too seriously (for instance, he says on one occasion that what he offers is "a kind of prophecy"), and he does communicate real insights in the course of his wild departures from literal Old Testament meaning. It is also perhaps easier to empathize with Origen, whose outlook is ultimately quite benign, than with Tertullian, who uses Psalm 110 as an address by an Old Testament "God of vengeance" promising Christ a share in his vindictive power. Cyprian is like a sergeant marshaling soldiers as he marshals Old Testament texts in an apparent attempt to prove that details of Christ's resurrection were foretold in the Old Testament.

Cyril of Jerusalem, like Origen, is mainly benign in his use of Old Testament materials; like Origen he uses them plentifully and especially favors the Song of Songs in his allegorizing. He has the Old Testament predicting the season (spring) and time (morning) of the resurrection, as well as the place (a garden) and other features. He sees the Jonah story as supplying detailed "proofs" for the possibility of the resurrection through Jonah's "resemblance" to Christ. Cyril invokes Christ's word in Matthew in support of the idea that his choice of "proofs" is a good one. But in the final analysis he says to his Christian hearers that he *believes* in the resurrection of Christ on the testimony of scripture and the testimony of the power of the risen Christ working "even at this day."

Chrysostom sees in the Old Testament an abundance of "sure signs," which he also calls "types." Ambrose is likewise cautious; he sees the second psalm ("You are my son. . . .") as a text that in Acts "appears" to refer to the resurrection. He uses features of the creation story and the psalms and Isaiah as contrasts and parallels and anticipatory statements. He goes further when he has the Church and Christ speaking through the Song of Songs, and angels and powers of heaven speaking through Psalm 24 and Deutero-Isaiah. Here he is rather clearly aware that he is allegorizing material addressed to a Christian audience in order to put his insights in rich scriptural perspective.

No Point in "Proof"

With the exception of Justin, none of these writers seem to be trying to really "prove" anything to a non-Christian audience in their use of Old Testament material. Often they use allegory to father illegitimate but sometimes useful meanings out of the Old Testament; at other times they merely apply or extend meanings they already find there. What follows from all this is that the use of the Old Testament to "prove" anything to an independent, uncommitted audience about the resurrection is a use that is limited in the fathers to such exceptional cases as Justin.

The resurrection is attested by "sure signs" from the Old Testament, Chrysostom says, but for proof of it we must go to the power of Christ in men. Similar thoughts are expressed by Origen and Cyril of Jerusalem. Chrysostom adds: "We believe that he arose. What reasoning can demonstrate to us the resurrection? None, but faith only." Augustine supports him on this: "Are you doubtful? . . . Remember that he is God; reflect that he is almighty. . . . Believe this, my brethren, for when it is a question of faith, it is not necessary to go on at length."

Christ Known by Faith

These fathers see the futility of attempting proof here. Reason cannot establish the resurrection—nor, if Ignatius is right, can any scripture. Ultimately there is only the knowledge of Jesus and the personally manifest power of his resurrection. This is a knowledge that is given through faith.

On this score, one of the great contributions of modern historical and literary research has been to force Christians away from "rational proof" and "proof through prophecy." (There may well have been no prophecy whatever—in the sense of clear prediction—before the resurrection, which is only to say that the resurrection in no sense need have been anticipated by "seers," and that the prophecies put into the mouth of Christ were not actually as clear as the gospels present them.)

Christ Today

Thus unburdened, the Christian is cast back upon faith and upon the testimony of the presence and work—in past and future history and at the present time ("this day")—of the risen and living Lord Jesus. "Without faith," as Chrysostom says, "it is impossible to know him."

Who Is This Lord?

We can then ask with Ambrose: "Who is this Lord of glory?" We have reviewed some of the fathers' answers. Here we can add some others, by way of a final tracing of the patristic picture of the risen Christ, whom the fathers universally see as the context of person and mystery in which men are called to live—now and forever.

He is the Lord who will come in majesty with his "saints," very like the Son of man of scriptural apocalypse (*Didache*). He is the assurance of the apostles as they move forth to preach the Good News of the coming kingdom (Clement). He is the new man, man's hope, apart from whom man has no real life, the living voice calling man to divine union (Ignatius). He is source of sublime joy (Polycarp). He is abolisher of death, preparer of a new people, revealer of the resurrection from the dead ("Barnabas"). He is eternal and heavenly high priest, beloved Son of the Father ("Martyrdom of Polycarp"). He is victor over demonic forces (Justin). He is God, Law, Word, king of Israel, liberator, ransom, king of men (Melito). He is Lord, God, savior and king; he is the new Adam and Son of Man, the one Son, the "one man" in whose human conquest of sin and death the father refashions all creation (Irenaeus). He is firstborn from the dead, first harvest of those who sleep, chief cornerstone of the new building of God—the new holy people; he is light of men and of the world, mighty Lord, moving transfigured in the crimson vesture of his passion (Origen). He is illuminator of the righteous (Hippolytus). He is triumphant restorer of man's flesh; in his resurrection he gives men his Holy Spirit (Novatian). He is giver of the Gospel; he rules from God's power, giving future life to men, whose body he will transfigure (Tertullian). He is resurrection and life for men; in him Christians abide, and in and through him they rise and reign forever (Cyprian). He is the man from heaven who came to change the earthly to the heavenly, bringing man to incorruption (Methodius). He is the very image of God himself, who came to renew mankind made after him in that image; he is the power of God and Word of God and true life itself, whose supreme purpose was the raising of man's body, and who on the third day raised up the temple of his own body—immortal, impassible and incorruptible—as the pledge of his human victory over death; he was and is God abiding with man for man's salvation (Athanasius).

Free among the dead, he delivers the dead and wears the diadem of death's conqueror (Cyril of Jerusalem). It was a war with death that he won, bringing man unending life; in him Christians daily rise again; in him their suffering finds dignity and meaning, for through it they know him and the power of his resurrection (Chrysostom). He is immortal and absolutely immutable, the bringer of the second age of immortality (Theodore). Unendingly he possesses the Holy Spirit and brings the indwelling Spirit into man; he is pioneer of man's entry into the new paradise; he is the divine man; through him men are transformed into his image (Cyril of Alexandria). He is the Son begotten on the day of the resurrection, in whom men are begotten as fellow sons of God in their baptism, their daily life and daily eucharist; he is the lamb in whose blood men are cleansed of sin; he is glorious in the white of Easter, a type of the baptismal robe, and glorious also in the now kingly crimson of his passion; he is lover and teacher of the Church, his bride, whom he leads into the inner mysteries (Ambrose). In his resurrection he brings man to justification and life; he is God; he is almighty; he solved the problem of man's double death (of soul and body) by his life, and he rose as symbolic sign and cause in the mystery of man's double resurrection: his spiritual resurrection now, and his physical resurrection which is to come (Augustine).

QUESTIONS FOR DISCUSSION

1. The *Didache,* the "Letter of Barnabas" and the writings of Polycarp, Justin, Irenaeus, Hippolytus, Cyprian and Tertullian tend to underline certain negative approaches. Give examples of these.

2. Indicate the positive concepts found in the fathers.
3. What two main conclusions are evident here?
4. How can people know Christ as risen Lord? How is he present in the world today?
5. Is it possible to prove the resurrection of Christ? Discuss.
6. What are some of the elements in the patristic picture of the risen Christ?
7. What is your impression of the fathers' teaching on the resurrection? Do you agree with the author's viewpoint on this-worldly resurrection?
8. Do you agree that Christ's resurrection provides a paradigm for the future of mankind?
9. Do you agree that Christ was born as Son at the time of his resurrection?
10. In what ways can we today go beyond the fathers in developing a theology of Christ's resurrection?

SELECTED READINGS

Basic Books on the Resurrection of Christ

Durwell, F. X., *The Resurrection.* New York: Sheed and Ward, 1964.

Ramsey, A. M., *The Resurrection of Christ.* London: Geoffrey Bles, 1965.

Stanley, D. M., *Christ's Resurrection in Pauline Soteriology.* Rome: Pontifical Biblical Institute, 1961.

Westcott, B. F., *The Revelation of the Risen Lord.* London, 1881.

Other Readings of Value

Fischer, B., "The Risen Christ and the Liturgy," in *Theology Digest* 8 (1960), pp. 123-26.

Gresch, P., "Protestant Theories Explaining the Redemption," in *Theology Digest* 5 (1957), p. 183.

Hick, J., "A Theodicy for Today," Part IV of *Evil and the God of Love.* New York: Harper & Row, 1966.

Vawter, B., "Resurrection and Redemption," in *Catholic Biblical Quarterly* 15 (1953), pp. 11-23.

Index

116